STERLING BIOGRAPHIES

# THOMAS A. EDISON

## The Man Who Lit Up the World

Martin Woodside

STERLING CHILDREN'S BOOKS
New York

# STERLING CHILDREN'S BOOKS
New York

An Imprint of Sterling Publishing
387 Park Avenue South
New York, NY 10016

STERLING CHILDREN'S BOOKS and the distinctive Sterling Children's Books logo
are trademarks of Sterling Publishing Co., Inc

© 2007 by Martin Woodside

Designed by Joshua Simons, Simonsays Design!
Image research by Susan Schader

ISBN 978-1-4027-3229-4 (paperback)
ISBN 978-1-4027-4955-1 (hardcover)

**Library of Congress Cataloging-in-Publication Data**
Woodside, Martin.
Thomas A. Edison : the man who lit up the world / Martin Woodside.
p. cm. -- (Sterling biographies)
Includes bibliographical references and index.
ISBN 978-1-4027-4955-1 (hardcover)
ISBN 978-1-4027-3229-4 (pbk.)
1. Edison, Thomas A. (Thomas Alva), 1847-1931--Juvenile literature. 2. Inventors--United
States--Biography--Juvenile literature. 3. Electric engineers--United States--Biography--
Juvenile literature. I. Title.

TK140.E3W58 2007
621.3092--dc22

2007003509

Distributed in Canada by Sterling Publishing
c/o Canadian Manda Group, 165 Dufferin Street
Toronto, Ontario, Canada M6K 3H6
Distributed in the United Kingdom by GMC Distribution Services
Castle Place, 166 high Street, Lewes, East Sussex, England BN7 1XU
Distributed in Australia by Capricorn Link (Australia) Pty. Ltd.
P.O. Box 704, Windsor, NSW 2756, Australia

For information about custom editions, special sales, and premium and
corporate purchases, please contact Sterling Special Sales at 800-805-5489 or
specialsales@sterlingpublishing.com.

Printed in China
Lot #:
6  8  10  9  7  5
10/13

www.sterlingpublishing.com/kids

# Contents

# Events in the Life of Thomas Edison

## 1847

**February 11, 1847**
Thomas Edison is born in Milan, Ohio, to Samuel and Nancy Edison. He is the youngest of seven children.

**1859**
Thomas starts working as a news butch on the Grand Trunk Railway. Eventually, he prints his own newspaper, the *Weekly Herald,* to sell on the train.

**March 1868**
Edison begins work as a telegraph operator at the main Western Union office in Boston, Massachusetts. He starts to sell some of his telegraphic inventions.

**October 13, 1868**
Edison registers his first patent, for an electronic vote recorder.

**April 1871**
Edison invents an improved stock ticker, which becomes a success.

**December 25, 1871**
Edison marries Mary Stilwell.

**December 29, 1875**
Edison buys a home in Menlo Park, New Jersey, and builds a new laboratory next to it. He eventually becomes known as the Wizard of Menlo Park.

**December 6, 1877**
Edison and his staff successfully test their phonograph, famously recording and playing back "Mary Had a Little Lamb." On December 15, Edison files his first patent application for the phonograph.

**October 1879**
Edison and his team discover a long-burning filament for his incandescent lightbulb.

**December 31, 1879**
Thomas Edison demonstrates his working incandescent lightbulb and lighting system to large crowds of eager sightseers outside of his Menlo Park lab.

**August 9, 1884**
Mary Stilwell Edison dies.

**February 24, 1886**
Mina Miller becomes the second Mrs. Edison in Akron, Ohio.

**May 21, 1891**
Thomas Edison purchases the Ogden Iron Company in Ogdensburg, New Jersey, which eventually fails.

**April 15, 1892**
The General Electric company is formed, merging Edison's company with the rival Thomson-Houston company.

**January 1894**
William K. L. Dickson produces the first motion picture to receive a copyright. By the end of 1894, Edison's team will copyright approximately seventy-five films.

**April 14, 1894**
The first commercial viewing of Edison's peephole kinetoscope is held in New York City.

**September 1900**
Thomas Edison suspends activity at his iron-ore operations, his greatest business failure. Edison will later recycle some of the machinery for use in cement and storage-battery businesses.

**May 27, 1901**
Thomas Edison organizes the Edison Storage Battery Company. By the following year, he's successfully road-testing electric vehicles equipped with his batteries.

**December 1903**
The Edison Manufacturing Company releases Edwin S. Porter's *The Great Train Robbery*, an important milestone in film history.

**May 1910**
Edison exhibits a scale model of his poured concrete house at a real estate exhibition in New York City.

**August 1926**
Edison steps down as the president of Thomas A. Edison, Inc., leaving his son Charles to oversee all of the business interests.

**October 18, 1931**
Thomas Edison dies in Glenmont, New Jersey.

## 1931

# The Persistent Inventor

*The most certain way to succeed is always to try just one more time.*

It was mid-October 1879, and Thomas Alva Edison had been working for five straight days and nights, hardly sleeping, hardly doing anything but laboring on his latest invention at his lab in Menlo Park, New Jersey. He was working on something that would top all his previous inventions—an electric lightbulb that would burn brightly for a long period of time. Edison knew he was close, and after more than a thousand tries, he was about to try it once more.

He had the power switched on. This time the lightbulb lit up and burned brightly for several hours! His persistence had paid off—he had produced a powerful **incandescent lightbulb**. This was the start of the modern electric age, and it would literally shine a new light onto the entire world. Edison's electric lighting was followed by a wealth of other inventions that would influence the entertainment and the industrial worlds. Throughout his lifetime, Edison welcomed each new challenge and always followed his simple philosophy to never give up. As he would often comment, "The most certain way to succeed is always to try just one more time."

# CHAPTER 1

# A Curious Child

*My mother was the making of me. She was so true,
so sure of me.*

Thomas Alva Edison was born in Milan, Ohio, in the
winter of 1847. He was the youngest of the seven Edison
children, and the third and final child born in America. His
parents, Samuel and Nancy, had moved to Milan from
Canada, and it didn't take long before the family was on
the move again. In his long and colorful life, Thomas
Edison would get quite used to traveling all over the world.

As a boy, Thomas loved to visit the town's busy
shipyards, to watch the men build the ships and watch

the ships come in and out on
the Milan canal. After
building the canal, Milan had
become a thriving town, and
Samuel Edison thought it was
the perfect place to start a
business. He built a house for
his family. He also set up a
mill to make roofing
materials, making full use
of the bustling canal to
ship them.

This 1853 photograph shows Thomas
Edison at age 3; he was the youngest of
7 children.

Milan's prosperity wouldn't last, though. Soon, the railroad would become America's best mode of transportation, but the people of Milan refused to let the train come through their town. Samuel Edison knew how foolish this was, and he decided to build his family's future elsewhere.

## A Lonely Childhood

Thomas, or Little Al, as his parents called him, was only seven when the Edisons took the ferry over Lake St. Clair to their new home in Port Huron, Michigan. He was a small, sickly boy and his parents worried often about his health. The doctor said that sickly Al was at risk for developing brain fever, and the young boy was already beginning to lose his hearing. Eventually, Edison would become completely deaf.

Edison was born and grew up in this two-story house, in Milan, Ohio.

As Al leaned over the railing, watching the boat cut across the smooth water of the lake, his long auburn hair fell over his eyes. No one who saw the young Thomas Edison then would have looked twice. Certainly, no one would have suspected that this frail child would become one of America's greatest inventors and one of its most powerful men.

Al faced a lonely childhood in his new home. Three of the Edison children had died young, victims of the brutal Ohio winters. His remaining siblings, William, Harriet Ann, and Marion, were much older. Marion had stayed with her husband in Milan, and Harriet had recently married as well. William was the only other sibling who moved into the new Edison house in Port Huron, but after a few months, he got a job and moved out.

The "house in the grove," as it came to be called, had tall ceilings and huge windows. It was a large white house perched on a low hill and surrounded by pine trees. There were six bedrooms and not nearly enough bodies to fill them. Samuel Edison constructed a one-hundred-foot-high tower on this property—one of his many schemes to make money. He called it "Edison's Tower" and charged twenty-five cents for the privilege of gaining access to the tower and its magnificent views.

Life became even lonelier for Al when his mother enrolled him

As a young boy, Thomas, shown in this c. 1850 photo, displayed a lively curiosity.

in the local school. Edison wasn't suited to the rigid structure of the one-room schoolhouse, and his stay there was not destined to last long. His teacher, Mr. Crawford, was a stern man who expected his students to learn the way he wanted them to learn. Al was easily distracted and restless, prone to drawing in his notebook instead of copying assignments. He asked a lot of questions and never seemed to follow directions, a situation surely made worse by his hearing problems. To Mr. Crawford this meant one thing—Thomas Edison was a bad student, and bad students had to be punished.

*He asked a lot of questions and never seemed to follow directions, a situation surely made worse by his hearing problems.*

Al spent many hours sitting on a stool in a corner. Mr. Crawford frequently mocked and struck Al in front of his classmates. One day, Al ran home crying, reporting that the teacher had said there was something wrong with his brain, and that he would never be able to learn.

Nancy became enraged. She told Al not to listen to Mr. Crawford and quickly pulled her son from school. She was an educated woman and had once been a schoolteacher. From then on she decided to see to her son's schooling herself. Edison later commented, "My mother was the making of me. She was so true, so sure of me."

## A Youthful Curiosity

Homeschooling suited the youngest Edison just fine. He was an enthusiastic reader, poring over book after book at an amazing pace, and he completed his mother's lessons easily. This left plenty of time for Al to satisfy his inquisitive nature, roaming through the big house and the surrounding country.

There are countless stories about Edison's youthful curiosity and the odd ways in which he tried to satisfy it. One famous story tells about the time he was discovered sitting on a nest of hen's eggs. When asked what he was doing, Al suggested that since the hen could get the eggs to hatch, so could he. Another time, he reasoned that if people ate like birds, they could fly like birds. After talking a friend into eating a concoction of mashed-up worms, Al was sorry to find that the only results of his experiment were an upset stomach and a harsh punishment.

Nancy Edison homeschooled her son Thomas and encouraged him to explore the world around him.

Edison spent countless hours collecting materials, which included chemicals as well as animal bones and feathers. These things took up so much space that Nancy urged him to set up his own simple lab in the basement. Exactly what sort of experiments Al undertook in this basement lab remains a mystery. Plenty of broken bottle glass and ceramics have been found at the sight of this first lab, though, sure signs that the young inventor was already quite busy.

By the age of twelve, Al was getting restless in the house in the grove. The Port Huron train station was just a few blocks away, and the sight of the trains coming

*Exactly what sort of experiments Al undertook in this basement lab remains a mystery.*

and going tempted his eager imagination. Once, Al took a train trip to visit his sister Marion back in Milan. His father came to fetch him and help with several large boxes that needed to be shipped to Port Huron. While waiting for the train, Al found a brush and some paint. He marked the family's name and address so neatly on the boxes that the stationmaster offered him a job on the spot.

Al turned the job down but soon had another more attractive offer. Every train had a "news butch" who sold books, newspapers, and food. His father helped him get that job on the Grand Trunk Railway, going from Port Huron to Detroit every day. Nancy was concerned about her young son being out on his own so much, but eventually she agreed to let the boy go. It was a big world and nothing could stop Thomas Edison from seeing it.

By the time Thomas was 13, he was working on the Grand Trunk Railway, which ran between Port Huron and Detroit, Michigan.

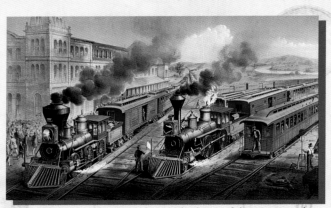

Samuel Edison knew that railroads were the future of the country, so he moved his family to Port Huron, Michigan.

## A Railroad Across the Country

The growth of the railroad was one of the most important developments of the nineteenth century. It made it much easier for people to travel and to ship commercial goods. The Baltimore and Ohio Railroad became America's first westbound railway in 1827, and the railroad expanded rapidly. In 1862, President Abraham Lincoln signed the Pacific Railway Act, providing money for the first transcontinental railroad, going all the way from one end of the country to the other. The Grand Trunk line began in Canada, but it soon extended service into the United States, and it included the line that young Edison worked on. By 1867, the Grand Trunk was the largest railway system in the world.

# CHAPTER 2

# A Young Entrepreneur

*The more to do the more done.*

At 7:00 a.m. the Grand Trunk pulled out of the station at Port Huron. The passengers were still settling in, finding their seats and putting away their bags. The industrious Al Edison had been at work for some time now. His tray completely loaded, he made his way down the aisles selling his goods.

It was a bumpy, three-hour ride from Port Huron to Detroit, and the only goods available on the train were the items for sale on the news butch's tray. Al was on his feet the whole time. He sold newspapers, magazines, candy, sandwiches, paperback novels, and whatever else his customers needed. Eventually, he sold fresh vegetables that had been grown on his father's land.

This late 19th-century wood engraving shows young Thomas Edison selling fruit, candy, and newspapers on the Grand Trunk Railway.

Thomas Edison printed his own newspaper while working onboard the Grand Trunk Rainroad. The small newspaper contained snippets of news, as seen in this copy from February 3, 1862.

Al had to spend almost the entire day in Detroit before the train headed back to Port Huron. Not surprisingly, he spent most of that time in the library, devoting long hours to reading as many books as he could. Thomas Edison would have read all the books in the world if he could have found the time, but there was always a train to catch. Al decided to narrow his focus, reading more and more science books, a sure hint of what lay in store.

## An Enterprising Young Publisher

In addition to the library, Al spent some time around the offices of the *Detroit Free Press*, which was one of the newspapers he sold on the train. He was curious to see how the paper-printing machines worked. After watching for a while, he had an idea. Using spare materials that the newspaper had thrown away, Al decided to print and publish his own newspaper!

Printing a newspaper on a moving train was no easy task, but Al practiced until he got it right. He put the letters for each and every word onto the small flat press himself, which he held on his lap. The end product was very simple (the size of a single piece of notebook paper), but Al was beginning to develop a good business sense. He knew that the people on the train were trapped there for hours. Many of them had probably already read the morning newspaper, and they needed something else to help pass the time. Edison called his paper the *Weekly Herald,* and it turned out to be quite popular. Focusing on local news and current events, his list of subscribers, Edison claimed, grew to five hundred.

Al set up a workshop in a small area in the back of the baggage car. This is where he stored his press and printmaking materials, along with the goods he sold as a news butch. Incredibly, Edison managed to run a third business. His fresh vegetables had become so popular that he opened a vegetable stand at the Port Huron station, hiring a couple of his friends to run it. Keeping busy would never be a problem for Thomas Edison. As he wrote in a headline for the *Weekly Herald*: "The more to do the more done."

Not all of his ideas were good ones, however. Al created a small laboratory in the baggage car and stored chemicals there. When he wasn't selling his wares or printing his newspaper, Al found time to conduct experiments in this mini-lab. As you might expect, one of these experiments went wrong, causing a small fire in the baggage car. The conductor was enraged, and Al quickly found himself thrown off at the next station with all the contents of his workshop.

A late 19th-century wood engraving shows the angry conductor throwing Al off the train after the young inventor causes an explosion with one of his experiments.

# A Fascination with the Telegraph

Young Edison managed to keep his job on the train despite this disaster. Still, he was starting to grow restless again. It was 1862 and he had become increasingly bored with his job as a news butch, often hiring his friends to do the work for him. He was fifteen years old now and feeling very grown up. He asked to be called Tom and began to think of bigger, more important jobs.

Tom eventually stopped publishing the *Weekly Herald* and started spending his days at the Mount Clemens train depot. Mount Clemens was a major hub on the Port Huron to Detroit line, and the stationmaster there was J. U. Mackenzie, who often let Tom listen in to the telegraph wires.

Tom was fascinated by the telegraph and the way it allowed people to communicate with one another even though they were miles apart. He sat in Mackenzie's office, listening to the busy flow of traffic over the telegraph wires and trying to learn as much as he could. The telegraph was an amazing **technology** back then. Soon, Tom would come up with ways to make the telegraph work better, and he later created new technology that would make the telegraph obsolete.

One morning, Tom was talking to Mr. Mackenzie outside the Mount Clemens station. Tom noticed that Mr. Mackenzie's three-year-old son, Jimmie, was playing on the tracks and a railway car was rolling straight toward him! The brakeman saw the boy but couldn't stop the car. Luckily Tom moved quickly, swooping the boy up and diving away from the oncoming train.

MORSE'S KEY.

The telegraph key, depicted in this 1873 wood engraving, was used to send messages through connecting metal wires.

Young Edison's dramatic rescue of Jimmie Mackenzie is brought to life in this 1879 wood engraving.

Neither Tom nor Jimmie were badly hurt, and Mr. Mackenzie was so grateful, he offered to teach Tom everything he knew about telegraphy.

## Becoming a Telegrapher

Tom learned quickly, and a few months later he got a job running the Western Union telegraph office, which was located in a jewelry story in downtown Port Huron. He worked long hours and even came back to the shop after dinner to practice on the machine. Tom had already started sleeping less, a habit that he would later become famous for. He tried to take small naps whenever he could, a few minutes here or there, sitting in a chair or lying under his worktable. Tom

*Tom had already started sleeping less, a habit that he would later become famous for.*

would sleep only four hours a night and probably wouldn't have slept at all if he didn't have to. The longer he was awake, the more work he could get done!

There was plenty of work in the telegraph office. The Civil War had started a year earlier, and the telegraph wires were buzzing with the latest news from the battlefront. Tom would listen anxiously as reports poured in about the victories, as well as the terrible losses, for both the North and the South.

After mastering his trade, Tom got a better job working as the telegrapher at Stratford Junction in Ontario, another stop on the Grand Trunk line. This was his first real job away from home, and Nancy was very sad to see her son go. Tom was sad as well, but he had big plans and he knew he couldn't stay in Port Huron forever.

For the next few years, Tom moved around frequently, finding work in telegraph offices at various train stations all around Michigan and the surrounding states. He liked to work the night hours best because they allowed him time to read, and he had his days to practice on the telegraph. Tom moved to the big city of Cincinnati and finally got promoted to a first-class operator.

Then, in 1867, Tom ran into some bad luck. At the age of twenty, he lost his job and ended up stuck back home in Port Huron. Tom was very sick that year and spent much of his time in bed. Things were looking bleak when a letter arrived from a friend he'd worked with at the telegraph office in Cincinnati. There was an opening at the Western Union bureau office in Boston, Massachusetts. It was a great opportunity and Tom jumped at it.

News from the field being sent by a telegraph operator during the Civil War is depicted in this 1862 drawing.

# Samuel Morse

Samuel Morse helped change the world with the invention of the telegraph. Morse imagined a device that sent messages through electric pulses from a moving train to the train station via telegraph wires. The device used electric **current** to stimulate an electromagnet that was attached to a marker, which would then make marks on a piece of paper. In 1838, Morse and his partners successfully sent a message two miles away. Soon he developed an entire system of dots and dashes for the telegraph, known as Morse code. In 1844, his new telegraph sent a message all the way from Baltimore to Washington, D.C.

Samuel Morse, in a photograph taken between 1855 and 1865, was the inventor of the telegraph.

Morse code was made up of different combinations of dots and dashes that represented each letter of the alphabet. Different configurations also indicated numerals zero through nine.

## MORSE'S ALPHABET.

| | | | |
|---|---|---|---|
| A · — | J · — — — | T — | 1 · — — — — |
| Ä · — · — | K — · — | U · · — | 2 · · — — · · |
| B — · · · | L · — · · | Ü · · — — | 3 · · · — — · |
| C — · — · | M — — | V · · · — | 4 · · · · — |
| D — · · | N — · | W · — — | 5 · · · · · |
| E · | O — — — | X — · · — | 6 — · · · · |
| É · · — · · | Ö — — — · | Y · — · — | 7 — — · · · |
| F · · — · | P · — — · | Z — — · · | 8 — — — · · |
| G — — · | Q — — · — | Ch — — — — | 9 — — — — · |
| H · · · · | R · — · | | 0 — — — — — |
| I · · | S · · · | Understood · · · — · | |

# CHAPTER 3

# On Becoming an Inventor

*Anything that won't sell, I don't want to invent.*
*Its sale is proof of utility, and utility is success.*

Nearly penniless and hungry for work, Tom traveled by train to Boston, slowed by a fierce blizzard that delayed his journey by four days. He showed up for his interview at the Western Union office in a dirty suit, still sick and pale. He got the job, though, impressing the superintendent with his willingness to go to work that very evening.

Thomas Edison registered his first patent for this vote recorder in 1868.

Boston was a big, busy place, but Tom was not intimidated. He continued his familiar pattern of working nights and studying during the day. He was glad to be working again but was tired of being just a telegraph operator and wanted to go into business on his own. His studies were all focused on science now, and particularly on electricity. Tom read book after book on electricity. The telegraph remained the most sophisticated tool that used electricity for communication. Tom knew that would change, and soon he would join a group of inventors who were racing toward the invention of a better and faster technology.

## Early Successes and Failures

Thomas Edison is famous for registering over a thousand **patents** in his career as an inventor. In Boston, he registered his first patent for the electric vote recorder. While at work, Edison had copied notes for congressional meetings and votes over the telegraph on numerous occasions. He knew how long and tedious the process of taking the vote count by hand was. Edison's device was meant to be installed at every representative's desk, and with the press of a button, a vote of "yes" or "no" could be instantly recorded.

*In Boston, he registered his first patent for the electric vote recorder.*

Edison found few takers for his invention. Although he would eventually become a shrewd businessman, this first venture failed. While the technology was good, the market was bad. The business of politics moved slowly, and most of the politicians liked it that way.

Failure didn't slow down the young inventor. In December 1868, he quit his job at Western Union and started his own

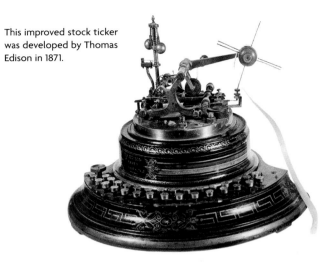

This improved stock ticker was developed by Thomas Edison in 1871.

business. Edison advertised himself in the paper as a "telegraph instrument maker." He did all kinds of work, including fixing and repairing telegraph wires, but he was very much an inventor at heart. The failure of the vote recorder had taught Edison a valuable lesson. Inventing wasn't enough. If he was going to make any money, he needed to invent something people would buy. He would later say, "Anything that won't sell, I don't want to invent. Its sale is proof of utility, and utility is success."

With that in mind, he turned his attention toward working on stock tickers. The stock ticker was an electronic device that businessmen used to keep up to date with the quickly changing prices on the **Stock Exchange**. Edison's stock ticker was an improvement on existing models in that it printed both letters and numerical figures. The product was successful, and Edison installed it in over twenty-five Boston business offices.

# Western Union

Western Union Telegraph grew from a small company in Rochester, New York, to become the biggest name in the telegraph business. By 1856, they were sending telegrams all across the country, and, soon, all over the world. The telegram became an increasingly important piece of technology. People used it not only to communicate information but also as a means to transfer money. Western Union introduced its money transfer service in 1871, and that became its primary business. Later, new technology like phones and computers replaced the telegraph, and Western Union changed with the times. In 2006, it closed down its telegram division.

The general operating department of the Western Union Telegraph building in New York City is shown in this c. 1875 photograph.

Edison had already established a pattern that he would follow throughout his life as an inventor. He worked incredibly hard, but he could never work on only one thing at a time. He made a habit of writing all his ideas down in one of his notebooks. By the end of his life, Edison had filled over three hundred notebooks, each one a jumble of new ideas alongside possible improvements for old ideas.

While making and selling his stock tickers, Edison had also been working on another project that he'd been thinking about for some time. He observed that there were limits to telegraph technology. Only one message at a time could be sent over the telegraph wire. That meant the lines were often busy, and the busier they got, the longer it took for messages to get through. Edison had a solution: find a way to send multiple messages at once, in more than one direction.

By 1869, Edison had put the finishing touches on a device designed for duplex telegraphy. The ambitious inventor put a lot of money into the project. He set up a highly publicized trial of the device, which was to send two messages between Rochester, New York, and New York City.

The results were unfortunate. The messages did not go through. Edison had not succeeded, and this time his failure was all over the news. What was worse was that he had invested most of his money in the experiment and now he was broke again. Penniless and disappointed, Edison didn't sound defeated. "I'll never give up," he said, "for I may have a streak of luck before I die." Instead, he was on the move again. Borrowing money for the train fare from a friend, Edison left Boston for the bright lights of New York City.

*Edison had not succeeded, and this time his failure was all over the news.*

# Edison Moves to New York City

When he got to New York City, Edison was twenty-two years old. He was struggling as an inventor, but his experiments with the telegraph had earned him a good reputation among those in the business. His biggest successes lay ahead of him, but for now, he was starting over again with no money, no job, and no place to live.

Good fortune brought Edison into contact with Dr. S. S. Laws. Doctor Laws had invented a device similar to Edison's stock ticker, which kept track of the fluctuating price of gold, and he had used this technology to set up his own business, tracking and reporting gold prices for investors. Doctor Laws

When Edison arrived in New York City, it was a busy, bustling town, as shown in this 1875 lithograph.

took a liking to Edison, but he had no job to offer him. Still, he let Edison sleep in the basement of his business headquarters in downtown Manhattan.

It was a humble start, but Edison moved up quickly. He soon mastered the equipment in the office and made a great impression on the chief engineer, Franklin Pope. Within months, Edison and Pope had gone into business for themselves, competing with Doctor Laws as well as maintaining and selling all kinds of telegraphic supplies.

The business did well, and Edison's services were in high demand. He left Pope and went into business on his own again, opening up a large workshop in Newark, New Jersey. By 1871, business was going quite well, but two important things happened that year that, although they had nothing to do with business, deeply affected Edison.

This photograph of Edison was taken c. 1878 when his fame as an inventor was spreading across the country.

# A Husband and Father

Mary Stilwell, photographed in 1871, married Thomas Edison on Christmas Day in 1871.

In April 1871, Edison got the sad news that his mother, Nancy, had died. With a heavy heart, he went back to Port Huron for the funeral. Coming back to New Jersey, Edison was distraught. He tried to console himself with his work, but something else caught his attention. Mary Stilwell was only sixteen when she had started working at the factory. She was a bright, lively girl, and Edison was interested in her right away. They met in the fall, and a few months later, on Christmas Day, the two were married.

After the wedding, the Edisons took a short honeymoon to Niagara Falls, but the restless inventor couldn't stand to be away from his work for long. Edison was still obsessed with multiple telegraphy and had some new ideas that he thought might just make it work.

Bringing those ideas to life required long hours in the lab, trying experiment after experiment until he arrived at just the right approach. In his Newark workshop, Edison finally put together a good mix of people and methods that he could work with. His laboratory team included Charles Batchelor, the first in a long line of trusted assistants. Batchelor and Edison worked closely together, getting nearer to perfecting a multiplex model

*In his Newark workshop, Edison finally put together a good mix of people and methods that he could work with.*

that could send two messages in two different directions at the same time.

This was the beginning of the most productive period of Edison's life. He worked day and night, often sleeping for brief spurts on a cot in his lab. This left little time for Edison to spend with his new bride. Balancing work and family would be a lifelong struggle for Edison. In 1872, Mary gave birth to the couple's first child, Marion. Edison was working frantically, with the quadruplex telegraph machine nearing completion, and Mary got used to tending to her young daughter alone.

*He worked day and night, often sleeping for brief spurts on a cot in his lab.*

Edison's neglect of his family caused him a lot of guilt. He wrote himself notes and made countless promises to himself to spend more time at home with his family. He was a **compulsive** worker, though, and simply couldn't put aside an idea until he'd worked it out to his satisfaction. Compounding that, of course, was the fact that he never worked on just one idea at a time.

Edison began to reap the rewards of his dedication to the quadruplex telegraph. His trials with the machine

Charles Batchelor was one of Edison's most trusted friends and workers.

were a success. Rather than produce the machines himself, Edison sold the rights to the **railroad baron** Stephen Jay Gould for $30,000, quite a remarkable sum at the time.

Edison had money and success now, but he was still restless. The Newark factory was too small and expensive. When Mary gave birth to the couple's second child, Thomas Jr., Edison decided that their house was too small as well. It was time to move, and he had found the perfect place. In 1876, Thomas Edison moved the family twelve miles away to the small farming town of Menlo Park, New Jersey. The town would become famous as the background for many of the inventor's greatest triumphs.

Marion Edison, shown here at age 8, was the first child of Thomas and Mary Edison.

# CHAPTER 4

# The Wizard of Menlo Park

*Genius is 1 percent inspiration, 99 percent perspiration.*

**M**enlo Park was ideal for Edison. The sleepy farm town provided the inventor with a distraction-free environment without being all that isolated. The Pennsylvania Railroad ran through town, and New York City was only twenty-five miles away. In 1876, Edison bought a large house in Menlo Park for his family and immediately started building his laboratory just a few hundred yards away.

This 1880 drawing of Menlo Park depicts Edison's home and lab, where he produced some of his most important work.

Once his laboratory was finished, Edison and his team began working on a hectic schedule—sometimes sixteen- to twenty-hour days. Edison's work methods were unusual for the time. Failure wasn't a problem for the hardworking inventor. In fact, it was part of his process.

He would put his team to work on thousands of experiments for even the smallest part of a project, running through every possible outcome before discovering what worked best. In the early days, other scientists criticized Edison for this, saying that his methods made for poor science. Edison would prove them all wrong, offering plenty of proof for his ferquently quoted motto: "Genius is 1 percent inspiration, 99 percent perspiration."

*He would put his team to work on thousands of experiments for even the smallest part of a project, running through every possible outcome before discovering what worked best.*

With the Menlo Park lab up and running, Edison was ready to do plenty of perspiring. He jokingly announced his goal of making a "minor invention every ten days and a big thing every six months or so." While that may have been a bit ambitious, the years at Menlo Park were good for Edison.

Edison started small. Together with Batchelor, he developed a device called an electric pen. This consisted of a needle driven by an electromagnetic motor, which could be set to stencil patterns through a piece of paper. Ink could be released then, filling in the stenciled pattern. Driven by Batchelor's aggressive salesmanship, the electric pen proved quite popular.

Thomas Edison's motorized electric pen was one of his first profitable inventions.

## The Telephone

In the midst of these heady times, Edison was shocked by the news that one of his rivals had beaten him to what would become one of the most important inventions of the century. Alexander Graham Bell took the technology of the telegraph to the next level, announcing in March 1876 that he'd successfully created the world's first working telephone. It was a landmark discovery and Edison was very jealous.

To Edison, Bell's telephone was a fairly rudimentary device. While it allowed two people to actually talk to each other over telegraph wires, there were limitations. Messages could be sent only over short distances. The transmitters, which sent and received the message on each end and made it louder, were of poor quality, and the speaker had to yell into the receiver to be heard.

# Invention of the Telephone

Picking up where the telegraph left off, the telephone **revolutionized** the way people communicated with one another. The telephone works by changing the sound of a voice to electronic impulses at one end of the phone and then turning the impulses back into something that sounds like the original voice at the other end. In 1831, Michael Faraday had proven that metal vibrations could be turned into electrical currents. Since then, a number of inventors had been working with the idea of the telephone.

While Alexander Graham Bell won the race, he did so by the narrowest of margins. Elisha Gray had been working on a telephone device at the same time as Bell. In fact, both men filed their patents the same day, February 14, 1876. Bell's telephone was slightly more advanced, and he filed his patent earlier, but only by two hours. In 1878, the first telephone exchange was set up in New Haven, Connecticut. In 1884, Boston and New York became the first two cities to be connected by the telephone. Soon, the technology spread all over the world.

Alexander Graham Bell is seen demonstrating his telephone at the 1876 Centennial Exposition in Philadelphia.

Edison figured that although he didn't make the first telephone, he would make the best telephone. He plunged into a bitter rivalry with Bell. This was another pattern of behavior that Edison would repeat throughout his career. He was a fierce competitor and would stop at nothing until he'd proven that he was right and that his invention was the best. Sometimes his stubbornness led to great successes. Other times, it cost him dearly.

*Edison figured that although he didn't make the first telephone, he would make the best telephone.*

Edison improved on Bell's telephone by devising a carbon and chalk transmitter for the receiver that produced a louder and clearer sound.

Edison worked closely with his Menlo Park team, shown here in 1880. Over the years, they conducted thousands of experiments under his supervision.

In the case of the telephone, there's little disagreement that Edison's transmitter was superior to Bell's. Edison conducted experiments with a number of different chemicals, trying to find the best material to increase the transmitter's ability to conduct sound waves through the phone line and into a second transmitter on a second phone. His near deafness made it difficult to conduct tests, but that hardly slowed him down. He came up with the amazing idea of biting down on a metal plate when he was testing the transmitter so he could feel the sounds traveling through his body.

After exhaustive testing, Edison found the perfect substance—the simple black carbon left by a burning lamp. (Carbon is a chemical element and a building block of many living and nonliving things on Earth.) Edison built two buttons out of the hardened carbon into the transmitter in the phone's receiver, which made the sound louder and clearer. Edison's carbon transmitter was a huge success. At Menlo Park, kerosene lamps were kept burning throughout the night so the burned-down carbon could be saved for making buttons the next day. Edison's lab worked around the clock to make the transmitters, which were sold to Western Union at a great profit.

## The Wizard Thrives in Menlo Park

Menlo Park was making a reputation for itself and becoming quite a place for moneymaking. Edison's team was getting bigger and better

The first song recorded on Edison's first phonograph was "Mary Had a Little Lamb."

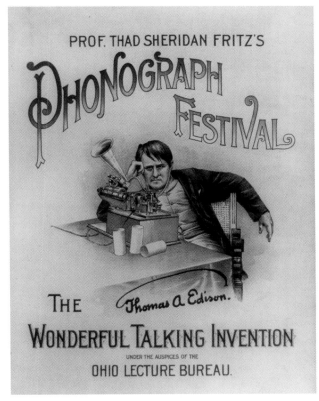

PROF. THAD SHERIDAN FRITZ'S

PHONOGRAPH FESTIVAL

THE *Thomas A. Edison.*

WONDERFUL TALKING INVENTION

UNDER THE AUSPICES OF THE
OHIO LECTURE BUREAU.

Thomas Edison is shown listening to his phonograph in this 1890 poster advertisement.

as people came from all over to work for him. The tiny town was filled with Edison's friends and family. Sarah Jordan, a distant relative, moved to town and established a boardinghouse nearby; it was populated largely by Edison employees or curiosity seekers, who came to see Edison and his lab. Reporters regularly came out from New York City to visit, and the papers nicknamed Edison the "Wizard of Menlo Park."

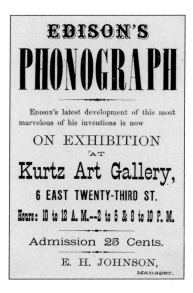

EDISON'S
PHONOGRAPH

EDISON's latest development of this most
marvelous of his inventions is now

ON EXHIBITION

AT

Kurtz Art Gallery,

6 EAST TWENTY-THIRD ST.

Hours: 10 to 12 A. M.--2 to 5 & 8 to 10 P. M.

Admission 25 Cents.

E. H. JOHNSON,

Manager.

A broadside poster in New York City, c. 1880, advertises a demonstration of Edison's new phonograph invention.

There was certainly plenty to report on at the Wizard's lab. Work at the lab went on at a furious pace, with a number of different projects going on at once. Two of these projects would earn a place among the most significant inventions of the century.

The idea for the phonograph came to Edison while he was working on the telephone transmitter. The telegraph could record electrical signals on a piece of paper through the indentations of a needle. The telephone transmitter could reproduce the vibrations made by sound waves. Edison imagined a machine that would combine elements of both devices, one that would reproduce sound vibrations and then record them.

Edison started out with a pretty good idea of what the device should be made of. There would be a diaphragm, or a

> *Work at the lab went on at a furious pace, with a number of different projects going on at once.*

vibrating disk, like the one in the telephone transmitter, attached to a needle that would indent sound vibrations on a piece of light paper. Edison was confident about this miraculous invention— maybe too confident. He boasted to the press, and a reporter from *Scientific American* announced that Edison's phonograph was finished before the inventor had even registered a patent.

After that, Edison and his team worked frantically for the next couple of weeks, trying to produce a working phonograph before his rivals could catch up to him. Finally he decided to replace paper with a piece of foil and set the foil to wrap around a cylinder. As the cylinder was turned, the needle made its marks on the foil, recording sounds.

For the first trial, Edison sang "Mary Had a Little Lamb" into the phonograph. The room was full of his workers, and they all gasped in excitement as the device played the song back, just as Edison had sang it. *"Mein Gott im Himmel!"* ("My God in Heaven!") exclaimed the German John Kruesi, one of Edison's inner-circle friends. Edison may have been the most surprised of all. He said, "I was always afraid of anything that worked the first time."

The phonograph made Edison famous all over the world. The reporters rushed to Menlo Park, clamoring for an audience with the great inventor. Edison was only too happy to oblige. He was a sharp businessman and did everything he could to call attention to his new invention. Edison performed tests for visiting reporters, set up theatrical demonstrations for the public, and put out a series of splashy advertisements. He repeated his performance of "Mary Had a Little Lamb," along with other children's songs and well-known poems.

> *The phonograph made Edison famous all over the world.*

Edison and his phonograph became the main attraction at a meeting of the National Academy of Sciences in Washington, D.C. He performed for senators, foreigners, and even had a private audience with President Rutherford Hayes. All were amazed by this incredible device that could record and play back the human voice.

## Balancing Family and Work

While Edison was basking in his fame, Mary was raising two children and was pregnant with a third. Thomas Sr. was rarely home, and Thomas Jr. was a sickly child requiring constant medical care. Marion, who was the oldest child and very lively, often made trips to visit her father in his lab down the street. Edison was always glad to be roused from his work, and he affectionately called his daughter "Dot" and nicknamed Thomas Jr. "Dash"—after the marks left by the telegraph. While "Dot" ran back and forth to her father's lab, Mary stayed at home with "Dash," growing lonelier and lonelier.

*While Edison was basking in his fame, Mary was raising two children and was pregnant with a third.*

Even when Edison took a vacation, he still kept working. In the summer of 1878, Edison joined a team of scientists who were traveling to Wyoming to observe a total **eclipse** of the sun. Experimenting with carbon for his telephone transmitters had, of course, given the inventor new ideas. One device he dreamed up was the tasimeter. Triggered by a carbon button, the tasimeter was intended to measure temperature changes as small as a millionth of a degree Fahrenheit. The eclipse offered the opportunity to test the tasimeter, and Edison promptly headed west for the July 29 event.

Edison saw the eclipse in Rawlins and successfully tested his tasimeter. Afterward, he continued on to California, riding the Union Pacific Railroad. Stephen Jay Gould had given Edison a special pass to ride the rails, and he made the most of it. His vacation lasted nearly two months, and he returned to Menlo Park before the fall, rested and ready. As far as the great inventor was concerned, there was still plenty of work to be done.

Thomas Edison (second from right) traveled to Rawlins, Wyoming, with an astronomy group in order to view a total eclipse of the sun.

# CHAPTER 5

# Let There Be Light!

*I believe I can beat you making electric lights.*

The lightbulb was Thomas Edison's most important innovation. It revolutionized the way electricity was used, and it created a thriving new industry that lit up city streets and houses all across America and the rest of the world. Edison had begun to seriously think of electric lighting during his vacation in the West. Watching a group of miners working near the Platte River, Edison wondered out loud to his companions: "Why cannot the power of yonder river be transmitted to these men by electricity?"

That question continued to interest Edison, and it wasn't long before he had his answer. Edison imagined not just an incandescent lightbulb, but wiring systems that could be installed to link thousands of the bulbs together so they could all be lit from the same power source. The businessman in Edison knew that the income from a project like that would set him up for a long time and free him from having to worry about anything but his inventions.

Edison also knew that he wasn't the first person to have this idea. In fact, many scientists and inventors were already at work on the problem of electric light and some

> *Edison imagined . . . wiring systems that could be installed to link thousands of the bulbs together.*

This image from the 1880s shows Jablochkoff's lights illuminating the Place de l'Opéra in Paris.

had made great progress. Paul Jablochkoff had already shocked the world in 1876 by inventing the Jablochkoff Electric Candle, which lit up the Avenue de l'Opéra in Paris, France.

The "candle" was really an arc light, containing two rods that glowed brightly until they burned down completely, much like a candle did. They were also loud and hard to control, spitting off bright showers of sparks. The arc light was certainly an improvement, compared to the dangerous **gaslights** that were used in street lamps at that time, but Edison dreamed of even bigger things.

In September 1878, Edison went to visit the workshop of William Wallace in Connecticut. Wallace was one of the leading inventors of arc lights, and Edison studied his work carefully.

## Jablochkoff Candle

Paul Jablochkoff's candle was a major invention and an important link in the chain of events that led to Edison's lightbulb. At the center of the design were two upright carbon rods. When they were connected with an electrical source, a brilliant light shone, which was ideal for outdoor lighting. The Jablochkoff candle was brighter than gas lamps and less expensive to make. This new invention, however, posed a serious threat to the gas lamp industry, at least until Edison came along with his incandescent lightbulb.

Russian Paul Jablochkoff, shown in this 19th-century engraving, invented the Jablochkoff Electric Candle, which was a stepping-stone toward Edison's incandescent lightbulb.

Wallace showed him a **dynamo generator** he'd made by hand, which created electrical energy and sent it out to a series of arc lights. Edison liked what he saw. He was confident now that his idea would work: Electricity could be distributed to light up not just tens but thousands of lights. He was also confident that arc lights were not the answer. "I believe I can beat you making electric lights," he announced boldly to Wallace. "I don't think you are working in the right direction."

## Work Begins on the Incandescent Lightbulb

At Menlo Park, Edison set out to find that right direction. Not for the first time, he was a bit overconfident, making fantastic claims to the press about his progress. "Of all the things that we have discovered this is about the simplest," Edison announced to the newspapers. He had barely begun work on the actual bulb at this point, and yet he was already promising to fill all of lower Manhattan with his electric lights! The great inventor's words caused plenty of excitement.

*"Of all the things that we have discovered this is about the simplest."*

The public was buzzing with anticipation, and investors rushed to put money into the project.

Edison had the money and the idea. Now people were ready for results, and the Wizard soon felt the pressure he'd helped create. There was also trouble at home. Mary was about to give birth to the couple's third child, and it was a difficult pregnancy. Since Edison's return from the West, Mary had become increasingly sick and anxious. She seemed depressed and had gained a lot of weight in the course of the pregnancy. But on October 26, 1878, she gave birth

Even with the birth in 1878 of Edison's third child, William, the inventor continued to spend long hours at his lab.

safely to their third child, William. Friends and family all breathed a sigh of relief. Eager to return to his work, Edison left his wife's side and returned to the lab before the day was over.

Edison was famous for the many hours spent in the lab, taking short naps when he became worn down. Mostly he worked, not bothering to eat or sleep for long periods of time. But the long hours weren't producing the results Edison wanted. He had the idea for the lightbulb worked out perfectly but was struggling to bring it to life.

*Edison and company would find out what others had tried and where they had failed.*

The basic components were simple. There was a wire that conducted the electrical current into a glass bulb and a fine material at the end of the wire that would light up when exposed to the electrical charge. How could the current be regulated, though? What material would hold the charge best? How should the glass bulb be designed?

Edison looked to answer these questions, and others, through his usually exhaustive methods. As the pressure mounted around him, the inventor decided he needed help. New members were added to the team—most important, Francis Upton. Upton was five years younger than Edison and well trained in mathematics. He went to work immediately, researching the history of lightbulb experiments and patents. Rather than start from scratch, Edison and company would find out what others had tried and where they had failed.

With Upton's thorough research, Edison started to put the particulars of the bulb together. The glass itself needed to be sealed because the intrusion of air could extinguish the light inside. Platinum was chosen instead of copper to go inside the bulb. In the spring of 1879, Edison managed to light a series of eighteen bulbs. The platinum inside the bulb was unreliable, though, and could not be kept burning for long periods of time.

## The Right Bulb Filament

Months dragged on and Edison and his team appeared stalled. They had managed to light plenty of bulbs, but they couldn't seem to keep them lit. Edison couldn't find the right **filament**, or thin strand, to use inside the bulb. It was in the fall of that same year when he came up with the solution of carbon, just like the lamp-blackened carbon he'd used to make his telephone transmitters.

Edison and his crew burned a simple piece of thread until it was carbonized. The thread was attached to the wire and placed

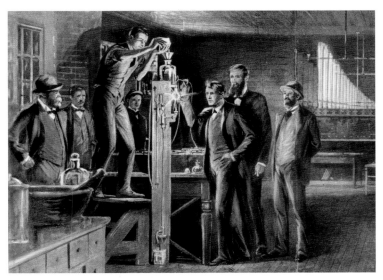

This drawing re-creates the break through in mid-October of 1879, when Edison and his crew successfully tested his long-burning incandescent lightbulb.

A replica of Edison's first incandescent lightbulb is shown in this 1879 photo.

inside the glass bulb. When the power went on, the thread gave off only a dull light and quickly died out. Tests showed that the carbonized thread was capable of handling a large amount of heat, so Edison knew he was on the right track. All the pieces were there, and he was close to putting them together.

Edison tried carbonizing a variety of materials, from wood to hair, and came to understand more and more about the carbonizing process. He decided to try simple thread again and managed to carbonize it more efficiently. Finally, in mid-October of 1879, Edison found success. With Batchelor, Upton, and the rest of the team looking on, Edison lit a bulb that burned brightly for more than thirteen hours.

Word spread quickly to Edison's financial backers, who had already created the Edison Electrical Company to sell Edison's bulbs and were nervous for results. At Christmastime, forty lamps were kept burning at Menlo Park from early morning until late at night. Huge crowds came to see the spectacle, and the newspapers wrote rave reviews of Edison's wonderful discovery. The Wizard had done it again, winning the race to make the first long-burning incandescent lightbulb. The bulb was just the first step, though, as Edison still had a lot of work to do to bring his dream of an electric city to life.

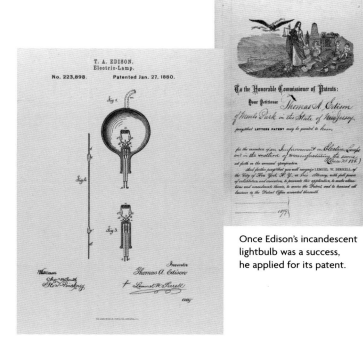

Once Edison's incandescent lightbulb was a success, he applied for its patent.

# CHAPTER 6

# The Business of Light

*I have accomplished all that I promised.*

Creating the lightbulb was an amazing accomplishment. It solidified Edison's reputation as an inventor, and it made him one of the most famous scientists in the world. The bulb was only part of Edison's master plan, though. The dream of the bulb came with a greater hope—that of connecting a large series of the lamps together to light homes, buildings, and city streets. In fact, before his lightbulb was even perfected, Edison was tinkering with ways to generate and divide power, creating whole systems that were to light up the streets of New York City.

In this 1878 cartoon, Thomas Edison and his new lightbulb reveal the true nature of the gas company's monopoly on the lighting industry; the two men are depicted with gas meters for heads.

# The Race to Light Up New York City

Most people didn't share Edison's vision. The gas companies were very powerful. Streets were lit by gaslights and most people expected they always would be. The development of the bulb turned many into believers of Edison's vision. Many of the inventor's rivals had been believers for some time, though. They knew the value of this new technology and the amount of money that could be made in developing it. Edison won the race to perfect the lightbulb, but now there was another challenge to confront.

Five rival companies had formed, hoping to **capitalize** on Edison's work and be the first to profit from it. Edison was determined to beat them. He'd promised to light up the city of New York, and he intended to keep his word. This mighty challenge would require Edison to be as good a businessman as he was an inventor.

Edison moved quickly, adding new people to his pool of assistants. Young Samuel Insull joined the team as Edison's personal secretary. Just twenty-one years old, Insull was shrewd and energetic, with a cool head for business. In 1880, he helped Edison's company file sixty patents, all of which became building blocks for the inventor's electrical empire.

Edison also came to an important agreement with Englishman Joseph Swan, who,

Some say that Englishman Joseph Swan, shown in this 1889 engraving, was the first to invent the lightbulb.

some argue, was the true inventor of the lightbulb. Swan was working with carbon before Edison ever was, and in 1879, Swan demonstrated a working carbon lamp. He was the first of many rivals who saw the power of the Edison name. The two men fought in the British courts, where Swan won out. Edison had vast power and resources, though, and the Englishman eventually joined forces with the great inventor, forming the Ediswan company in London.

Foreign markets were important to Edison. New York was just the start; he wanted to light up the whole world! With that in mind, Charles Batchelor was sent to Paris to establish Edison's company there and prepare for the Paris Electrical **Exposition** of 1881. Edison shipped a massive generator overseas, and Batchelor oversaw the installation of a display of electric lights that wowed the crowds. Edison was laying the groundwork for a vast electrical empire.

At the Paris Electrical Exposition in 1881, Edison's electric lights amazed the crowds.

# Illuminating Manhattan

Meanwhile, the Wizard concentrated on keeping his promise to the people of New York. The city skyscape was already a maze of telegraph and telephone wires. Many thought the situation was quite dangerous, and in fact, a few workers had already met a grisly end, coming in contact with broken electrical wires and getting electrocuted. Edison intended to bury the wires safely underground.

By the end of 1881, Edison had a system he thought would work. He'd created a massive generator that weighed twenty-seven tons and was powerful enough to light up more than one thousand lights! He figured out how to subdivide the electricity as well, using a number of smaller wires to feed

The Manhattan office of the Edison Electric Illuminating Company is shown in this 1881 photograph.

into one main wire. This was important because the copper used for the wire was very expensive and subdividing saved a lot of money. The system was ready; now all Edison had to do was convince the city of New York to let him dig up its streets and put that system into place.

Edison moved his business into a four-story brownstone in Manhattan, calling it the Edison Electric Illuminating Company.

Edison's electric generator is represented in this 1879 illustration.

By the summer of 1882, Edison and his business **ventures** had taken over a number of buildings throughout the city. Two buildings on Pearl Street were among his most important acquisitions. These would be the center of his lighting system downtown—power stations housing two massive dynamo generators that would feed lights for a square mile all around.

Taking advantage of the rave reviews from the Paris exhibition, Edison secured the help of influential financial backers, such as banker J. P. Morgan, and finally received permission to dig the trenches for his electrical wires. The digging went on at night, while by day Edison's labs worked to make the wires and bulbs. Piece by piece the complicated system was put together.

Edison had surged ahead of the rival companies and was well on his way to winning the race to bring lights to the streets of Manhattan. By the autumn of 1882, the signs of success were evident. Parts of the downtown area near Pearl Street had gone

## J. P. Morgan

John Pierpont Morgan was one of America's most powerful men. He founded J. P. Morgan and Company, which became one of the wealthiest banking houses in the world. Before that, Morgan accumulated a great deal of wealth through railroads, and eventually gained control over more than half of all the railroads in the country. In 1882, Edison installed three hundred lights in Morgan's lavish Manhattan mansion. This helped promote Edison, and for a while Morgan was one of his chief financial backers.

Financier J. P. Morgan was one of Edison's most prominent financial supporters.

electric. When Edison threw the switch that powered those lights, he remarked, "I have accomplished all that I promised."

Edison had also brought electric lights indoors, installing a full set of lights in J. P. Morgan's mansion. This was a huge story for the press and made the public even more excited about the idea of electric lights. Edison the businessman was proving to be just as successful as Edison the inventor.

# A Death in the Family

While his business ventures were thriving, things were getting bleaker in Edison's neglected home life. Mary's health continued to worsen as she sank further into lonely depression. Keeping house and raising three children all alone was overwhelming, and on doctor's orders, Edison had the family moved to the Clarendon Hotel on Fourth Avenue.

*While his business ventures were thriving, things were getting bleaker in Edison's neglected home life.*

But things kept deteriorating. Edison found time in his busy schedule to finally take Mary on a brief vacation to Florida. Their rest was short-lived, and they returned to the news that Mary's father was quite ill. It was 1884 and Edison stood by his wife as her father passed away that spring.

The death was an ominous sign of things to come. Mary got sick again and was confined to her bed back in Menlo Park. Edison spent his days worrying over her, and his nights sneaking away to his lab in New York. While at the lab, Edison got the devastating news that Mary's condition was serious. On August 9, just short of her thirtieth birthday, Mary Edison died.

Edison was desolate. Work was his passion, but his family was dear to him—his source of safety and stability. As summer turned to fall, Edison found himself all alone, the sole parent to his three children. Business pressures were building up around him as his rivals in the electricity game had gotten stronger. The next few years would prove difficult, and Thomas Edison would have to face some of the stiffest challenges yet.

# CHAPTER 7

# New Challenges

*Mina Miller Edison is the sweetest little woman who ever bestowed love on a miserable homely good-for-nothing male.*

In the wake of Mary's death, Edison plunged back into his work. He was getting more involved with business dealings than with inventions, building up his electric company and fighting the ever-growing ranks of his competitors. These business ventures were quite profitable, but life without Mary was lonely and difficult.

In the winter of 1884, Edison met Mina Miller at a technology exposition in New Orleans. Mina was only nineteen years old and the daughter of Ohio businessman Lewis Miller, who had made a fortune developing and improving farm equipment. Edison was immediately infatuated with Mina, but this time he'd have to wait. Mina wasn't about to rush into marriage; in fact, she was already being courted by another man, whom she

Mina Miller became the second Mrs. Edison in 1886.

This 1948 image shows Edison's winter home in Fort Myers, Florida.

thought would eventually become her husband. Still, Edison was convinced he had met the right woman to marry, and as usual, he was determined to pursue what he wanted until he got it.

After New Orleans, Edison took another short vacation to Florida. His oldest child, daughter Marion, had become his constant companion. The trip to Florida provided them both with some much-needed relaxation and helped greatly to revive Edison's spirits. Edison developed a strong affection for the lush landscape and mild weather he found in Florida. Without hesitation, the inventor invested in property, buying a thirteen-acre piece of riverside property just outside of Fort Myers. As usual, the purchase was motivated as much by business as by pleasure. Edison enjoyed sunny Florida, but he also liked the ready availability of bamboo, which he'd begun to use inside his lightbulbs.

Back in New York, Edison focused on his two main goals—establishing the dominance of his electrical empire and finding a new wife and mother for his children. From 1885 to 1900, more than two hundred lawsuits were filed against Edison's company, attacking nearly every part of his electrical system, from the lightbulb itself to the supporting equipment that powered it. With all of the costly court battles, Edison was fortunate in his success with the lightbulb. The creation of an effective way to use it to light city streets had made him a very rich man.

## A New Wife and a New Lab

It was the summer of 1885, and Edison's feelings for Mina were growing stronger. He wrote and visited her often. Finally, after a few months of this, he proposed to her.

Edison had been teaching Mina to use Morse code. Legend has it that Edison, on a car trip to New England, was sitting in the backseat with Mina and he tapped a marriage proposal on her hand. Whether the story is true, Edison definitely proposed to Mina that summer, and in September he wrote to Lewis Miller to ask his blessing for the marriage. The blessing was granted, and Thomas Edison was set to be married a second time.

*The blessing was granted, and Thomas Edison was set to be married a second time.*

Before the wedding, the great inventor purchased a magnificent twenty-nine-room estate, called Glenmont, in New Jersey. It would be the perfect place for Edison and his new bride. Thomas Edison married Mina Miller on

In an undated photograph, Edison is shown working in his West Orange lab.

February 24, 1886, at the bride's home in Akron, Ohio. Edison was nervous in the days up to the wedding. At one point he became terribly frightened that the minister would not speak clearly, and with Edison's defective hearing, he would not be able to hear his words. The wedding was a success, though, and afterward the newlyweds set out for Florida.

Unsurprisingly, even his honeymoon failed to be a real vacation for Edison. As soon as his wife got situated, the busy inventor went right back to work, spending large portions of the day in the makeshift lab he'd assembled on the grounds of his new Florida property. By 1887, Edison purchased land in West Orange, New Jersey, and was beginning work on a magnificent new lab complex. Although Edison seemed to, once again, place work above family, he expressed his admiration for Mina in a note that read, "Mina Miller Edison is the sweetest little woman who ever bestowed love on a miserable homely good-for-nothing male."

These were interesting years for Thomas Edison. He was happily remarried and the head of a thriving new business. As an inventor, though, Edison was entering a rough period. One of Edison's great flaws was his stubborn pride. If he had an idea, it was hard for him to admit that someone else might have a better one.

*One of Edison's great flaws was his stubborn pride. If he had an idea, it was hard for him to admit that someone else might have a better one.*

Fierce competitiveness drove Edison to success in some cases, as with his race to design a better telephone than Alexander Graham Bell. At other times it really hurt him, as it did with Nikola Tesla and the idea of **alternating current**.

## A Worthy Competitor

Born in Croatia, Tesla grew up in a farming village. Like Edison, Tesla was a **visionary** and a genius, and he would become one of the most important inventors ever to work with electricity. But unlike Edison, Tesla was something of a dreamer. He was more concerned with ideas than with the practicality of making them work or creating a profit.

The physical appearance of the two men showed just how

different they were. Edison was short and frumpy. He dressed
in workman's clothes and had little use for fancy things. Tesla
was tall and thin. He had expensive taste in clothes and wore
the newest and fanciest suits. When the two men met, Edison
quickly nicknamed the young Tesla "our Parisian," because of
his fancy wardrobe.

It was in Paris that Tesla first went to work for the French
affiliate of the Edison Electrical Company. Charles Batchelor
hired him in 1882, and Tesla worked in Europe for two years.
Batchelor noticed how talented his young employee was, writing
to Edison that, "I know two great men. One is you and the other

# Nikola Tesla

Nikola Tesla's ideas about electricity were just as significant as Thomas Edison's, and some would say even more so. Tesla is most famous for working with alternating current, for which he sold the patents to George Westinghouse in 1888. In 1891, Tesla invented the Tesla Coil, which converted electricity into a high-frequency, high-voltage form and pumped it out into the air. This would become an important factor in the later development of radios and televisions.

Tesla was very interested in harnessing the power of electricity without wires. He was famous for daring displays where he would light lightbulbs in his hand without wires, just by letting electricity pass through his body. Tesla also conceived of the earth as a giant conductor of electrical current; he thought this idea could be used to light whole cities with no wires at all. In his experiments, he succeeded in lighting lamps as far away as twenty-five miles. He was a poor businessman, and the lack of money prevented him from exploring many of these ideas. When he died, in 1943, most of his concepts remained in the notebooks where he'd dreamed them up.

In an undated image, Tesla is shown generating artificial lightning in his laboratory. Edison disagreed with him on the merits of alternating currents.

An undated illustration shows the dynamo room at Edison's Pearl Street Station.

is this young man." That was high praise indeed, and in 1884, Tesla headed across the Atlantic Ocean to join Edison's operation in New York.

Edison had always been smart about using the talents of his employees to further his own inventions. None of those employees were as talented as Tesla, though. Perhaps the great

*For whatever reason, Thomas Edison couldn't accept Tesla's idea of alternating current, and that decision came back to haunt him.*

inventor was jealous of the young man. Perhaps he didn't trust him. For whatever reason, Thomas Edison couldn't accept Tesla's idea of alternating current, and that decision came back to haunt him.

At the heart of the lighting system that Edison created for New York City, and of other systems that he had designed, was the use of a direct current power source. With direct current, power was sent out from the generator and then returned back to the generator. The **voltage** stayed the same and had to be kept fairly low to avoid damaging the lamps and houses it flowed into. This worked just fine when the current was traveling only a short distance, as with the Pearl Street Station in New York City. When it came to sending current out for longer distances, this system was not very effective. Alternating current provided an answer to this problem.

*In this case, Edison's vision proved quite limited. He turned a blind eye to alternating current and scoffed at Tesla's ideas.*

Tesla had been thinking and dreaming of ways to use alternating current long before he came to America to work with Thomas Edison. Alternating current flows back and forth continuously, with the voltage building up to a high point then changing directions and going back, where it builds to another high point. This kind of current could be sent over long distances. When it came to building bigger electrical systems that would spread out over larger areas, alternating current was clearly superior to direct current.

At the time Tesla went to work for Edison, no one had come up with an effective system for managing alternating current. Many in the scientific world laughed at the idea, the same way people had laughed when Edison suggested that gaslights would soon be replaced by electric ones. But Tesla wasn't laughing. He believed in alternating current. He knew it could work.

In this case, Edison's vision proved quite limited. He turned a blind eye to alternating current and scoffed at Tesla's ideas. It didn't take long for the young inventor to leave Edison's company and strike off on his own. By 1888, he had made great strides toward developing an alternating current generator. Edison wouldn't accept Tesla's revolutionary ideas, but Edison's competitors did—most important, George Westinghouse.

Westinghouse, originally from upstate New York, had struck it rich in Pittsburgh by making a lot of money on the railroads. Slowly, he'd been getting more deeply involved with the business of electricity, buying up patents and setting up his own company to rival Edison's. Westinghouse hired Tesla and made alternating current the heart of his power system. By 1889, Westinghouse had become Edison's main competitor, setting up over one thousand power plants across the country.

*Westinghouse was beating Edison on the market, and Edison's financial backers were getting uneasy.*

Edison didn't take the threat seriously at first. By the time he did, it was too late. Alternating current worked, but Edison still refused to use it. Instead he went on the attack, claiming that alternating current was unsafe and always would be. Edison even got involved with the

# George Westinghouse

Born in 1846, George Westinghouse spent his youth building farm machinery for his father. Unsurprisingly, Westinghouse grew up to be an inventor. He developed air brakes that made trains much safer, and in 1869, he formed the Westinghouse Air Brake Company. After continuing to work with trains, Westinghouse saw the great potential in electricity, and in 1886, he formed the Westinghouse Electrical Company. The company's accomplishments included building generators to harness the electrical power of Niagara Falls, and developing the first alternating current engine for trains.

George Westinghouse, in an early 1900s photograph, was one of Edison's leading competitors.

development of the first electric chair for executing criminals, which used alternating current, taking the opportunity to rename it "death current."

These efforts were of little use. Westinghouse was beating Edison on the market, and Edison's financial backers were getting uneasy. Edison stubbornly went on refusing alternating current, believing that direct current could compete with it. This would eventually cost the great inventor more than he could have ever imagined.

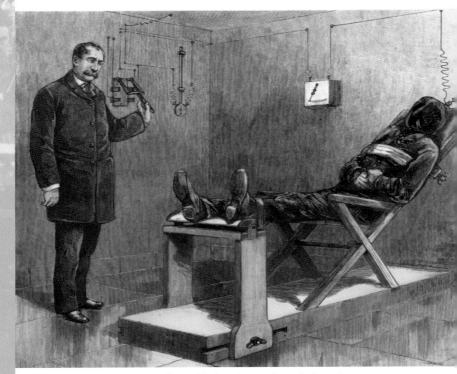

An 1890 engraving depicts the world's first electric chair, which used alternating current.

# CHAPTER 8

# Bitter Ends and New Beginnings

*They are trying to steal my invention.*

While his electrical business was struggling, Edison was hard at work on other projects, which involved dreaming up new ideas and dusting off old ones. He was also building a family with his young bride, a family that grew large quickly and demanded the kind of attention Thomas Edison was never good at giving. These were busy years for Edison.

## Competition and Cutthroat Deals

As early as 1885, Edison turned his attention back to the invention that first made him famous. The phonograph still ranked as one of his most important inventions. But when Edison plunged into his experiments with electricity, he left the phonograph behind, and others took advantage, making advancements in the technology that surpassed what Edison had done.

Edison's old rival Alexander Graham Bell was the most notable of these innovators. Bell had been amazed by Edison's invention and studied it carefully. By 1887, Bell, along with his cousin Chichester Bell and associate Charles Tainter, developed an improved version of Edison's phonograph called the graphophone. It was powered by electricity and used wax-covered cardboard, instead of tinfoil, to record and play sounds. The design was superior to Edison's, and Bell's financial backers were eager to put the machine out on the market.

Bell respected Edison as the inventor of the phonograph, and he didn't want to take advantage of his fellow inventor. He approached Edison to suggest that they go into business together, marketing the new phonograph under both men's names. Predictably, Edison's competitive nature got the best of him. He was outraged by Bell's proposal. "Those fellows are a bunch of pirates," he complained. "They are trying to steal my invention."

As far as Edison was concerned, anything Bell did, he could do better. With his fully equipped new lab and a capable, hardworking staff, Edison wasted no time in setting out to prove exactly that. He spent much of 1888 hard at work perfecting his new phonograph. Like Bell's machine, Edison's device was powered by an electric motor and it recorded on wax. Edison's machines also started using cylinders made completely of wax, so that once a recording had become worn out, the wax could be shaved off and the cylinder used again.

BELL-TAINTER MACHINE
ENTERED IN CATALOGUE AT THE
NATIONAL MUSEUM, NOV. 30, 1920
MUSEUM CATALOGUE NO. 287853.

Improving upon Edison's phonograph, Alexander Graham Bell came out with his graphophone, which is shown in this photograph.

This c. 1892 photograph shows Edison seated in the center, surrounded by his lab technicians, who helped perfect his wax-recording phonograph.

Edison's new phonograph worked much better than his old one, and he moved quickly to start profiting from it, both in the U.S. and in England. He faced stiff competition from Bell and his American Graphophone Company. Not only did Bell have a head start, but he was suing Edison for violating patent rights by using wax for the phonograph's new cylinders. The stage was now set for a long and expensive legal battle. But before that played out, Edison was tricked into joining his business with Bell's.

Jesse H. Lippincott was a Civil War veteran who'd made a profitable business out of manufacturing drinking glasses. He created the North American Phonograph Company and made a generous offer to buy out Edison's Phonograph Company. Edison stood to make a lot of money from selling the rights, and he soon agreed to the deal. What he didn't know was that Lippincott was secretly negotiating with Bell at the same time, hoping to combine both companies under his control. By the summer of 1888, the deal was complete. When Edison found out what was happening, it was too late. He made a lot of money but was furious and bitterly disappointed that he'd been deceived. He brought the issue to court, eventually regaining control of his beloved phonograph.

Returning to the phonograph had provided Edison with an important glimpse of the future. He had always thought of the phonograph as a business tool—something that would be used for taking dictation and recording important meetings. Neither he nor Bell—nor anyone else for that matter—realized how much money could be made from marketing the phonograph for entertainment. After selling out to Lippincott, Edison started to see these new possibilities, and he took steps toward exploring them.

*Neither he nor Bell— nor anyone else for that matter—realized how much money could be made from marketing the phonograph for entertainment.*

In 1888, Edison came up with the idea of a talking doll, one with a small phonographic device built inside of it that could record and repeat what was said to it. The idea proved to be far superior than the design, as the dolls were too fragile and many of them ended up getting broken when they were shipped. More significantly, while working on the phonograph, Edison started to think about making movies; about ways "to

Edison invented a talking doll that held a phonograph device in its torso.

devise an instrument which should do for the eye what the phonograph does for the ear." A few years later, Edison would begin working more intensely on this amazing idea.

## A Growing Family and an Absent Father

In the meantime, the Edison family continued to grow. On May 21, 1888, Mina gave birth to the couple's first child, and Edison's fourth, daughter Madeleine. A father again at forty-one years of age, Edison had often been absent during his wife's pregnancy. Typically, he spent most of his nights working in the lab. A year later, he took Mina with him to Paris for the Universal Exhibition, which featured a huge display dedicated to Edison's inventions.

This undated photo shows Edison with his wife, Mina, and daughter, Marion, who eventually became estranged from her famous father.

In this print, Edison demonstrates his phonograph at the 1889 Universal Exhibition in Paris.

While Edison basked in the attention from his colleagues and admirers, Mina found less to enjoy about the trip to France. She was constantly worried about baby Madeleine, who was back at home in Glenmont. In Paris, Mina got in touch with her stepdaughter, Marion. The sixteen-year-old had been touring Europe and she met her parents in Paris. Unfortunately, there was great tension between Mina and the precocious teenager, which seemed to have worsened over the years. At the time of the exhibit, however, Edison remained oblivious to these family problems.

Edison enjoyed the summer in Paris immensely. He met scientists from all over the world, and perhaps most important, he met the French scientist Étienne-Jules Marey. Marey had been experimenting with photography and he showed Edison the pictures he'd taken of animals in motion. Marey sped the pictures up to sixty frames per second to give the illusion that they were actually moving. These photos helped Edison greatly in imagining how to construct his motion picture camera.

# Étienne-Jules Marey

Important early work in motion pictures was done in France. In 1878, Eadweard Muybridge set twelve cameras up with trip wires to show whether a horse's hooves left the ground when it galloped. This inspired Étienne-Jules Marey to construct his "photographic gun" that could take up to twelve photographs per second of bodies in motion. Marey's main interest was in the study of flight. He looked at how insects and birds flew, and used his "gun" to further these studies. He improved the device by creating a camera that could record multiple images on the same camera plate. For Edison, this was only the beginning: this helped him envision a camera that could capture moving pictures.

Étienne-Jules Marey, shown in his lab, influenced Edison's inventive mind and his first motion picture camera.

## Business and Betrayal

Back in America, Edison's electric companies continued to struggle. Westinghouse and others were having great success with systems that used alternating current. Edison's financial backers were getting more and more worried. When it was clear that they couldn't change Edison's mind about alternating current, they eventually decided to change his role in the company. In

Henry Villard, shown in this late 1800s photograph, helped oversee the merger of the Edison General Electric Company.

1889, the Edison General Electric Company was formed, initially combining seven of Edison's businesses into one. Friend and businessman Henry Villard helped Edison oversee this merger, which made the inventor quite a bit of money. In early 1892, Villard oversaw another move (this one without his friend's blessing), merging Edison Electric with rival company Thomson-Houston. Edison's longtime supporter J. P. Morgan approved the merger, and shockingly, Edison was removed from the head of the company he'd created.

The papers were abuzz with the news of Edison's removal, and the great inventor was stunned, furious, and deeply hurt. It was certainly a great defeat. Edison was lauded as the inventor of the lightbulb, and he'd made his name—and a lot of money—with it. Now, he'd been betrayed—by Villard and his old friend Sammy Insull, who took an executive position with the new company.

# CHAPTER 9

# Rough Waters

*I'm going to do something now so different . . .
people will forget that my name ever was
connected with anything electrical.*

Edison's loss of his electric company left him bitter and defiant. He walked away, announcing, "I'm going to do something now so different and so much bigger than anything I've ever done before that people will forget that my name ever was connected with anything electrical."

The matter of iron had been in Thomas Edison's thoughts for a long time. As early as the 1870s, he had mentioned to his colleagues how scarce iron ore was, especially in the eastern part of the United States. Edison was reminded of this problem, once he had plunged into the electricity business, as his dynamos were made mostly of iron.

## Too Stubborn to Quit

It didn't take long for the busy inventor to come up with a solution. Edison found that beach sand had a high iron content and that by passing a magnet over the sand he could separate the iron out. By the early 1880s, Edison had patented this separating process and formed the Edison Ore-Milling Company. The company had a brief and unsuccessful run before going out of business—a sign of things to come.

Of course, failure only made Edison try harder, no matter how difficult things became. His stubbornness was so great in the case of his mining operation that it became known as "Edison's Folly." There are a number of theories about what kept Edison going despite numerous failures. Many of his friends and coworkers thought that Edison kept on because of his bitterness and anger over losing the electrical company he started, which made him eager to succeed at something completely different and prove his critics wrong.

At first, things went fairly well. Edison made enough money from his work in electricity so that he didn't need outside investors. An entire ore separation room had been added to Edison's lab, and he continued to develop his separating machinery. He put scientist and photographer William K. L. Dickson in charge of much of the work at the lab. Edison also looked outside of his lab for answers, and hired the mining expert John Birkinbine in 1888.

Working together, the men developed a machine that was more effective than any competing technology, with a massive magnet—some six feet long and ten inches thick—driving the system. Edison would most likely have brought a happy end to his adventures with iron ore if he had decided to sell this machinery to existing mining companies. Instead, he decided on a far more reckless and costly path.

*Working together, the men developed a machine that was more effective than any competing technology.*

While Dickson and Birkinbine were working in the lab, Edison was dreaming of big possibilities for his new technology. The inventor embarked on a mad buying spree, collecting

This 1895 photograph shows a worker standing on the Corliss engine, which was used as a power source at Edison's Ogden mine.

mining rights for thousands of acres of eastern land. The largest of these sites was in Sparta, New Jersey, near the village of Ogdensburg. This would become the busy center of Edison's mining operation. Eventually, more than three hundred workers came to populate the rural area. Edison even managed to have a post office established, and the town was renamed Edison.

The Ogden mine featured expensive machinery that took years for Edison to perfect. Huge masses of rock were shattered by explosives and removed by a massive steam

## Iron and Steel Industry

The expansion of the railroads and the **Industrial Revolution** made iron production very important. Wrought iron was made by removing impurities from the iron ore. The more impurities that could be removed, the better the quality. Steel was sturdier than wrought iron, but it was very expensive to make. In 1856, Henry Bessemer developed an inexpensive way to make steel by using molten iron. And with the perfection of the Bessemer process, the steel industry grew rapidly. Steel production became a major business in the United States, and there continued to be a great need for iron ore, which Edison tried to capitalize on by creating the Edison Ore-Milling Company.

This 1876 engraving shows the manufacturing of steel by Bessemer Steel.

shovel onto railway cars. The rocks were then crushed, and the iron ore was separated out, using a complicated and largely automated process.

Edison's boastful claims of success and a busy marketing team had quickly drawn the attention of several buyers, but he was behind schedule from the start. The machinery kept breaking, and production was often stopped while workers made repairs. By 1891, the mine was running at full speed and filling orders for hundreds of tons of iron ore. Due to the large operating costs, the mine was also losing thousands of dollars each month.

## More Family Problems

Things were going badly for the great inventor's new business venture. Edison's children continued to struggle as well, particularly the three from his first marriage. Edison's favorite child, Marion, grew more and more distant. After joining the family at the Paris exposition, "Dot" continued to travel through Europe, contacting her father only when she needed money. She was increasingly melancholy and became terribly ill, coming down with a severe case of smallpox. Recovering in Dresden, Germany, Marion felt sad and lonely and, worst of all, ignored by her famous father. While Marion

Thomas Edison Jr., shown here at age five, and his brother, William, both struggled with their father's frequent absences.

Glenmont was Edison's estate in West Orange, New Jersey.

lay in bed for nearly a month, Edison managed to write her only twice. Afterward, Marion found the scars left by the smallpox traumatizing, and the treatment she had received from her father to be even more painful.

*Marion found the scars left by the smallpox traumatizing, and the treatment she'd received from her father to be even more painful.*

Marion's younger siblings, Tom Jr. and William, were having their own difficulties closer to home. Edison, even though often absent, cast an imposing shadow. Being the son of Thomas Edison left a lot to live up to. As a youngster, Edison himself had struggled badly in school, but when Mina sent his boys away to a rigorous prep school that neither boy was cut out for, Edison didn't protest.

With their mother gone, and their father's lack of attention, Tom Jr. and William struggled on their own. Both boys found the prep school to be a cold and hostile place. Tom wrote home with a catalog of physical ailments, developing a sense of inadequacy that would continue to grow in later years, while William begged to come home and be allowed to go to public school. With their father busy in his Ogden mine, both boys addressed their letters to their stepmother.

Mina had become quite settled as the domestic center of the Edison clan. She gave birth to her second child, and Edison's fifth, Charles, in 1890. Eight years later, Mina and Edison had another son, Theodore. In 1891, the inventor put the Glenmont estate officially in Mina's name. The symbolism was clear: The lab, and all the inventions that came out of it, would be Edison's domain, while the domestic world would belong to Mina. Despite this symbolic agreement, home life and business were both complicated and messy during this time. Edison's struggle with Mina and the children from his first wife had just begun.

*The symbolism was clear: The lab, and all the inventions that came out of it, would be Edison's domain, while the domestic world would belong to Mina.*

# CHAPTER 10

# Making Pictures Move

*In the year 1887, the idea occurred to me that it was possible to devise an instrument which should do for the eye what the phonograph does for the ear . . .*

Thomas Edison never had to worry about being stuck on only one idea at a time. And so, even as his iron-ore venture was fast becoming a disaster, he was pushing ahead with another remarkable invention.

Edison wasn't the first person to create motion pictures, just as he wasn't the first person to work on the incandescent lightbulb. Once again, though, Edison saw the potential in the idea before most people did, and he worked quickly and relentlessly to make it a reality. Edison turned to William K. L. Dickson again to help in the lab. Both men were still primarily concerned with the iron-ore business, and work on motion pictures went slowly at first.

## The Kinetoscope

After his visit to the Paris exposition and his exposure to Marey's work, Edison had a clearer vision. He imagined a camera that worked along the lines of the old telegraph machines, with the film running in long bands between two moving reels. Individuals could record and play back images in the same way music could be recorded and played back on the phonograph. When the Wizard returned to his New Jersey lab, he found that Dickson had built a special building for motion picture experiments and was making good progress.

By 1891, Edison and Dickson had made some amazing strides in developing their camera. Edison filed a patent for the device in July of that year, and Edison saw that as only the beginning. He also filed a patent on the kinetoscope machine used to play their recorded pictures; this was a coin-operated boxlike device with a peephole. Edison imagined the kinetoscope as something like the coin-operated phonograph he had already developed and sold.

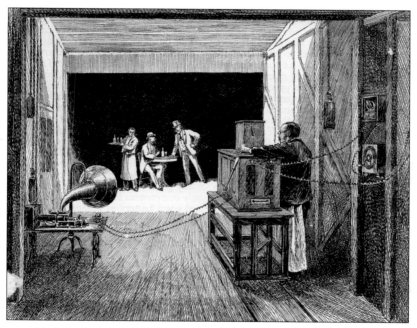

An undated drawing depicts the inside of Edison's kinetograph theater, where he recorded his moving images.

Edison's first motion picture studio, shown in this photograph, c. 1899, was called the Black Maria.

Outside of his work with motion pictures, 1891 brought mixed results for Edison. With the death of Jesse Lippincott, he was able to regain control of his phonograph company. The iron-ore business continued to be a personal and financial disappointment.

Still, the great inventor was proving that he was far from washed up. He was spending more and more of his time on the motion picture business. Dickson had constructed a strange-looking building named the Black Maria on the grounds of Edison's West Orange lab. This odd-shaped building was a studio for making films. It was lined with black paper and set on a circular track. The whole building could be moved

*He was spending more and more of his time on the motion picture business.*

to change with the direction of the sun. Part of the adjustable roof could be opened and closed to control the amount of light allowed in. The World's Fair in Chicago was less than a year away, and Edison was eager to have a working kinetoscope ready by then, along with films to play on it.

As usual, Edison was being a bit overambitious. It wasn't until 1894 that Edison formed a film company as part of the Edison Manufacturing Company and his motion picture business was in full swing. The first twenty-five kinetoscopes were completed and shipped out that year. Once again, Edison was at the head of a major technological breakthrough.

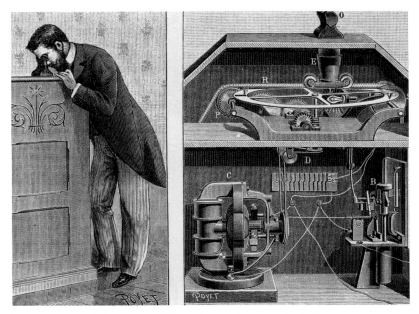

A man looks through the viewer of this kinetoscope to see moving pictures.

# A Better Moving Picture Machine

Edison had gotten off to a strong start with motion pictures. His vision for the future of the industry was a bit hazy, though. The great inventor concentrated most of his energies on perfecting the kinetoscope. Dickson was left with the responsibility of making the actual films. Sales for the machine were good at first but began to drop off quickly. Edison's familiar stubbornness was coming back to haunt him. Movie viewing developed into what we know today, with groups of people watching movies projected on large screens, rather than watching them separately on individual machines. Edison rejected this idea and insisted that his kinetoscope would be the future.

This c. 1899 photograph shows how the Biograph Company was set up at the Coney Island clubhouse.

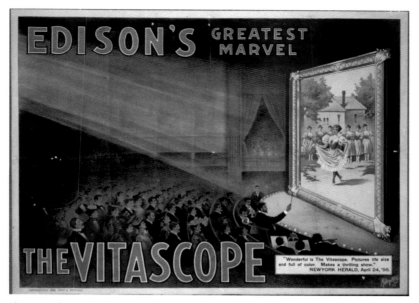

This 1886 ad promotes Edison's Vitascope, which projected moving images onto a large screen that groups of people could view together.

Sales of the machine continued to fall. Other competitors were already having success developing both motion picture cameras and movie **projectors**. Dickson saw the potential of projectors, and he was becoming frustrated by Edison's stubbornness. He finally parted ways with his employer and joined an Edison competitor with whom he developed a projector called the Biograph.

Edison eventually saw that he was fighting a losing battle. He hadn't done any work on developing a projector and had to look for outside help. He hired Thomas Armat and acquired the rights to Armat's projection device. Edison eventually renamed this the Vitascope. Armat was willing to let Edison put his name on the machine, knowing that with the Edison name attached, success would likely follow.

The makers of the Biograph projector and the Vitascope engaged in tough competition—in the film business as well as in the courtroom. Edison finally received his patent for the kinetoscope in 1897, and he immediately took legal action against Biograph, claiming that it violated his patent.

*He quickly took action, building a new movie studio in New York City.*

It took ten long years before the lawsuit was finally resolved, in Edison's favor. A lot had happened during that time. The beginning of a new century started off poorly for the great inventor, who finally had to shut down his struggling Ogden mine in 1902. The victory against the Biograph provided much-needed good news for Edison. He quickly took action, building a new movie studio in New York City. While he remained fixated on the development of the technology rather than the content of his movies, he proved shrewd once again finding outside help. He hired Edwin Porter to handle the production and directing of his films.

With Porter at the helm, Edison's company remained at the forefront of the growing motion picture business. As the years passed, Edison stayed away from the creative side of his film company, while Porter created numerous films that were quite successful. In 1903, he came out with *The Great Train Robbery*, a ten-minute movie that was a huge success and became an important milestone in the history of filmmaking.

# Edwin S. Porter

Edwin S. Porter emigrated from Italy to America in 1895. He worked for Edison's Vitascope company from 1896 to 1898, left to work as a projectionist, and then returned to Edison's movie company in 1900. Porter made mostly documentary films but had a breakthrough when he completed *Life of an American Fireman*. The director cleverly mixed footage of firefighters with scenes he had written and staged. The film was successful and this encouraged Porter. He made *The Great Train Robbery*, based on Butch Cassidy and his 1900 train robbery in Wyoming, which was the first movie western and one of the most important achievements in film history. Porter continued to make movies after leaving Edison's company. He formed his own production company, and his work was hugely influential on the development of narrative filmmaking.

This movie still is from Edwin Porter's *The Great Train Robbery*, which had a running time of ten minutes.

# CHAPTER 11

# New Ideas and Old Problems

*I never quit until I get what I'm after.*

The new century saw a new breed of scientists emerging. Coming out of the universities, these highly trained professionals placed more emphasis on mathematics and scientific theory than did self-schooled inventors like Edison. The public still saw Edison as the "Wizard of Menlo Park," the man who had **conjured** up amazing inventions like the lightbulb and the phonograph. To the new breed of scientists, Edison and his methods were more a part of the past than of the present.

Edison's failure in the iron-ore business certainly didn't help boost his reputation. Also, many of his longtime coworkers had moved on or retired. By the end of his iron-ore venture, even his valued friend and assistant Charles Batchelor was fading out of the picture, working less and spending more time with his family. Neither criticism nor old age slowed Thomas Edison, though. As he headed into his golden years, Edison continued to come up with new ideas and find ways to make them work.

At the turn of the century, Edison's lab was arguably as busy as it had ever been. The Wizard had more than one hundred people on his staff who continued to work on the phonograph and record new material for it. Additionally, he developed two new successful projects—one involving batteries and the other involving cement.

## The Edison Storage Battery

Edison had been curious about the potential of storage batteries for some time, and the automobile boom revived his interest. While it may seem hard to believe now, early automobiles ran on electricity, not gasoline. These cars were quite expensive, and it wouldn't be long before cheaper gas-powered automobiles would take over. But Edison thought that electric cars could be affordable and effective if he developed a reliable storage battery to help power them.

This photograph shows Edison with one of his storage batteries.

An undated photograph shows Edison promoting his battery in a Bailey electric car. The sign reads: "1000 Mile Endurance Run Bailey Electric New Edison Storage Battery."

Storage batteries had a much longer life span than the batteries that had been used in the telegraph and other electric devices. They could be charged and recharged before completely dying out. The more often the battery could be recharged, the more valuable it was, and Edison was determined to develop a storage battery that had a very long life.

The main obstacle to this was **corrosion**. Storage batteries created positive and negative electrical charges, and the electrodes that received these charges had to be made of a substance that wouldn't corrode too easily. Edison and other scientists working in this field became stuck on this problem.

# Electric Cars

Robert Anderson of Scotland invented the first electric carriage in the 1830s. Countryman Robert Davidson, working with American Thomas Davenport, improved Anderson's creation, and they were the first to use non-rechargeable electric cells. Starting in the 1860s, serious work went into developing storage batteries, and electric cars grew in popularity. In 1899 and 1900, electric cars actually outsold all other types of cars in America. Steam- and gasoline-powered vehicles were also being developed, but the electric models were the most efficient and manageable.

As the roads connecting cities and towns improved, people began traveling greater distances, which the electric cars could not easily accommodate. They continued to be popular until Ford perfected his gas-powered Model T. With Ford's assembly-line production of automobiles, the price of his cars dropped dramatically. By 1912, the average electric car sold for about $1,700 while Ford's car carried a price tag of about $650.

It was extremely difficult to find a substance that would resist corrosion and still have a long life, while at the same time be lightweight and affordable.

Starting in 1899, Edison and his associates went through a laborious process of trial and error, trying to find just the right metal. They worked with zinc, copper, iron, cadmium, and nickel, among others, to see which would work best without being too expensive. By 1901, Edison thought he had his solution. He filed patents for a battery using iron and nickel, and formed the Edison Storage Battery Company to sell it.

Despite Edison's failure with the iron mine, he didn't have any problems raising money for his new company or getting the public excited about his new invention. By 1904, when the Edison Storage Battery Company was pumping out a full line of storage batteries, a sizable buzz had been built up around the inventor and his latest creation.

In this photograph from 1910, Thomas Edison Jr. is driving his father in an electric car.

Edison is shown talking with a lab associate, in this 1906 photograph.

In the usual fashion, Edison had declared success a bit early. There were still some kinks to be worked out, and it took a few more years before he and his lab actually perfected their storage battery. Edison Storage Battery did a brisk business nevertheless, and Edison's work with the battery turned out to be quite profitable. If not for the advances of gas-powered automobiles, which soon captured the country's imagination, it might have been even more profitable.

# The Cement Business

Another Edison success came out of his failed iron-ore mine. While the mines had been operating, Edison had made some money by selling the separated sand to cement companies. Toward the end, when it was clear that his iron-ore business was going to close down for good, Edison started to look into other ways to make money. The answer was in cement.

*Another Edison success came out of his failed iron-ore mine.*

Natural cement was made by heating limestone, and engineers had been tinkering with the best formula for this by experimenting with different ingredients. In 1824, Joseph Aspdin invented Portland cement, which was an artificial cement made by mixing clay with chalk and heating it in a limekiln. In Edison's time, Portland cement was just starting to emerge as an alternative to natural cement. Once again, Edison saw the possibilities for marketing Portland cement before most of the world did, and he went to work trying to realize those possibilities.

Edison started his cement plant in 1899. He thought that the method of heating the cement was the most crucial part of the process, so he developed and built a 150-foot-long rotary kiln made of cast iron. It took a few years to get the kiln working right. The process was slowed down in 1903, when a tragic fire broke out, resulting in the death of some of Edison's workmen. Edison closed down the plant and reorganized it so that it would operate more safely and efficiently.

A few years later, Edison's cement works were up and running again, producing a high-quality brand of Portland cement. The profits were still small. Running a large industrial operation meant dealing with many problems, such as maintaining expensive machinery and paying for frequent repairs. His work with cement was a success, though, and it gave Edison some interesting ideas.

One of these ideas was to make concrete houses by pouring cement into iron ore. Edison thought this inexpensive method would make it possible for working-class people to own homes. Although he never explored the idea fully, he made a few sample houses in Union, New Jersey, in 1919, some of which are still standing today.

The long rotary kiln that Edison developed was probably the most impressive thing to come out of his dabbling in the

This 1919 photograph shows a cement house being built in Union, New Jersey.

cement business. It proved to be far more effective than the kilns that had previously been used to make cement, and long after he had left the cement business, this technology continued to be quite important.

## Deteriorating Family Relations

Despite "Edison's Folly," the Edison name continued to represent success and brilliance to both the public and the business community. For the three children from his first marriage, however, the Edison name was more of a curse than a blessing. Marion eventually returned home from Europe

*For the three children from his first marriage, however, the Edison name was more of a curse than a blessing.*

in 1892, after recovering from smallpox. Her father was distant, and when she came to visit once, he even refused to see her. Eventually, Marion returned to Europe, where she married a German army lieutenant, Kark Oscar Oeser. After that, Edison's once beloved "Dot" stayed out of the United States—and away from her father—for more than twenty years.

In some ways, neglect was the best thing that Edison had to offer the three unfortunate children from his first marriage. While Marion ran away, Tom and William continued to struggle in their father's shadow. Tom kept floundering in school and didn't have much better luck in the working world. He tried working for his father at the mine in Ogden but was dogged by feelings of inferiority. "I don't feel I would ever be able to talk to you the way I would like," the demoralized Tom wrote to his father, "because you are so far my superior in every way that when I am in your presence I am perfectly helpless."

After leaving Ogden, Tom tried with little success to go into business on his own. He was often swindled by businessmen who were eager to use the famous Edison name to sell worthless products for a quick profit. Tom embarrassed his father with these schemes, and Edison warned his son against these kinds of con artists. In 1899, Tom shamed his father again, when it was revealed that he had secretly married a chorus girl. Edison turned his back on his son, and Tom's new wife soon did the same; she had married the younger Edison to capitalize on his name and money, and not out of love.

By 1903, things were looking dark for Tom, when he ended up in a sanitarium. But he ultimately ran into some good fortune there, when he met his nurse, Beatrice Heyzer, with whom he fell in love. After Tom left the sanitarium, he and Beatrice got married. Edison's oldest son had finally found some happiness, but Tom wanted no part of his famous name; he took on an assumed name, and the couple became known as Mr. and Mrs. Burton Willard.

*Edison's oldest son had finally found some happiness, but Tom wanted no part of his famous name.*

Young William didn't have it quite as rough as his brother, but he also struggled to live up to his father's expectations. He was swindled

Thomas A. Edison Jr. changed his name to Burton Willard to avoid the pressures of his family name.

a few times, as Tom had been, into using the Edison name for shady business ventures. In 1899, William also wed, against Edison's wishes, a farmer's daughter named Blanche Travers. Like his older siblings, William felt the sting of his father's neglect, as the famous inventor broke off relations with his young son as punishment.

*Like his older siblings, William felt the sting of his father's neglect, as the famous inventor broke off relations with his young son as punishment.*

Later on, the two reconciled. Still, Edison was of little help to William when he attempted to go into business, making and selling a type of spark plug he'd developed for cars. The spark plugs had potential, but Edison refused to give him money or use his connections to help, believing that William should make it on his own, just as Edison had done so many years before.

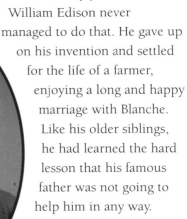

William Edison never managed to do that. He gave up on his invention and settled for the life of a farmer, enjoying a long and happy marriage with Blanche. Like his older siblings, he had learned the hard lesson that his famous father was not going to help him in any way.

Even though William Edison, shown here at age 19, married against his father's wishes, he nevertheless had a long, successful marriage.

# CHAPTER 12

# A Dwindling Empire

*No one who has a normal ear can hear as well as I can.*

Edison's neglect of his three oldest children is sad, but perhaps not shocking. Work always took first place for Thomas Edison. Still, when it came to Mina and the children from his second marriage, it seems that Edison tried to be a better husband and father. Madeleine, Charles, and Theodore had an easier time of things,

Edison poses with his wife, Mina, and two of their children, Madeleine and Charles, in this photograph taken between 1890 and 1910.

This late 19th-century photograph shows Edison and one of his sons on a fishing trip.

benefiting from the full attention of at least one parent—their loving mother, Mina. Edison became an attentive father in his later years as well, spending more time with the family and taking more frequent trips to their Florida summer home.

Retirement was never a real option for the busy inventor, although he did slow down, abandoning the business side of his companies to concentrate on his work in the lab. In 1911, Edison tried to simplify his business interests by combining them all under the name Thomas A. Edison Incorporated. He planned to spend more time with his loved ones, becoming something of a new man—one who would spend more time fishing off the pier at his Florida vacation home than catching catnaps on the cot in his lab.

# Edison's Phonograph

Edison might have been able to stay away from the lab more often if it hadn't been for the phonograph. The phonograph had always been Edison's baby—his first big invention—and one that he'd continued working with since his early days. It was close to his heart, and he'd fight for it until the end.

As Edison entered his sixtieth year, the phonograph was experiencing some tough times. Edison's company had struggled through the country's economic depression of 1907 and run into some stiff competition. The gramophone, made by the Victor Talking Machine Company, was Edison's main competitor, and its sales were strong. There were several reasons why the Victor machines were becoming more popular than the phonograph.

In this 1897 photograph, a family is listening to Edison's phonograph, but by the early 1900s, the phonograph was being outsold by its rival, the Victor gramophone.

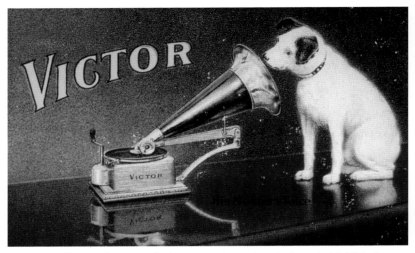

The Victor Talking Machine, one of Edison's main competitors, is shown in this 1906 ad, which features Nipper the dog as part of its logo.

The Victor machine played a disc, very similar to the records some people still use today, as opposed to the cylinder, which was central to Edison's device. German immigrant Emile Berliner had done work similar to that of Alexander Graham Bell in developing his original gramophone disc some twenty years earlier. By the turn of the century, Berliner had made significant improvements to the gramophone. The discs were being made of wax, offering a sound quality comparable to Edison's cylinders. The Victor company also offered a varied line of machines to play Berliner's discs, in a range of prices, and this gave the gramophone a clear edge over the phonograph.

Edison fought hard to revive his phonograph. The inventor had experimented with disc recordings as early as 1877, but he'd decided the future of the phonograph lay with the cylinder. Even with the success of the gramophone, the inventor was slow to change his mind. He was reluctant to give up the cylinder, and he and his lab staff worked diligently to make one that would be superior to the Victor disc. Long hours in the lab finally paid off. In 1912, Edison introduced a new plastic coating for his cylinders called Blue Amberol. Edison was delighted with the sound quality of these cylinders, which he found superior to any of his competitor's discs. Still, the cylinder could only play for four minutes, maximum, while his rivals had already developed discs that could play for more than ten minutes. The Blue Amberol cylinders may have had the best sound quality, but the public had moved on, and gramophone sales far surpassed the sales of Edison's new cylinders.

*Your neighbors could not tell which is the real voice of Mlle. Verlet*

If Alice Verlet, of the Paris Opera, stood on your verandah, or near an open window, and sang in direct comparison with Edison's Re-Creation of her voice, your neighbors could not distinguish one from the other, nor could you, unless you watched Mlle. Verlet's lips.

*Mlle. Verlet* of the Paris Opera, famed Belgian Coloratura Soprano, is but one of many great artists who have proved by direct comparison that Edison's new art re-creates all forms of music so exactly that the Re-Creation cannot be detected from the original.

Hear Edison's Re-Creation of the voice of Alice Verlet; then hear the great Belgian artist herself when she is on tour.

*Edison's New Art*

re-creates all forms of music so perfectly that the Re-Creation cannot be detected from the original

*Read what music critics say, after hearing the direct comparison made*

"Mlle. Verlet gave several numbers, and it was indeed difficult to determine except by watching her lips just when she ceased to sing in person, so flawless are her recorded numbers."
—*Albany Journal*, N. Y., October 9, 1915.

"The audience did not know whether the music came from her or the instrument."
—*Syracuse Post-Standard*, February 11, 1916.

"The effect was marvelous."
—*Chicago American*, November 30, 1915.

"Indistinguishable from that of her visible self."
—*Kansas City Times*, November 30, 1915.

*The* **NEW EDISON**

is not a talking machine. It embodies a new art whereby all forms of music are actually re-created. It is not alone Alice Verlet's voice which is so re-created. No voice is beyond this new art.

**THOMAS A. EDISON, Inc.** Dept. 237 B
Orange, N. J.

In 1916, Edison, like his competitor, used the singing stars of his time to sell his "New Edison" phonograph.

A new direction was needed. While Edison perfected his Blue Amberol cylinders, his associates kept pushing him to begin designing discs. Edison was never an easy person to push, but by late 1909 he began to experiment with discs. One way or another, he was determined to develop a product that was superior to the Victor machine. By the end of 1912, the first Edison disc phonographs were released. Edison had developed a disc that he claimed was long lasting and nearly unbreakable. Edison also made other improvements to his phonograph, introducing the diamond needle that would become a standard for later-day record players.

*Edison also made other improvements to his phonograph, introducing the diamond needle that would become a standard for later-day record players.*

Technology wasn't Edison's only problem. Victor boasted an impressive catalog—full of big-name recording artists—which was another key reason for his competitor's impressive sales. Edison designed his phonograph to play only Edison discs and continued to emphasize his superior technology, saying, "I propose to depend on the quality of the records and not the reputation of the singers." This attitude, and the incompatibility of Edison's machine with other discs, hurt sales, as many people preferred the music available on Victor. By 1917, Edison was still fighting a losing battle.

Eventually, Edison decided to start selecting the musicians for his company by himself. The great inventor was nearly deaf, but he claimed that this actually gave him an advantage. He revived the incredible technique he had used when he'd worked on perfecting the telephone: biting down on a piano while it was being played. Edison claimed that this allowed him to feel the musical notes, giving him a better sense of their purity than if he simply used his ears. In fact, Edison claimed that "no one who has a normal ear can hear as well as I can."

In the competition against Victor, the inventor's business sense proved as effective as his technical innovations. Edison worked hard to improve the quality of his phonograph and the variety of musicians in his catalog. He worked just as hard launching a massive advertising campaign to promote his new phonographs. Edison created a buzz with his

*Edison worked hard to improve the quality of his phonograph and the variety of musicians in his catalog.*

Viewers line up to view the newest moving pictures at this Kinetoscope arcade in San Francisco.

Tone Tests, which set up a live performer and an Edison phonograph playing on a darkened stage. The audience listened to both and was challenged to tell the difference between the recording and the "real thing." Edison's 1915 film *The Voice of the Violin* featured a Tone Test by the famous opera singer Anna Case.

## Divided Attentions

While Edison immersed himself in the phonograph, his motion picture business was doing poorly. Part of this can be traced to the inventor's divided attentions. More important, the success (or lack of it) of Edison's films had a lot to do with the quality of his collaborators. Edison's vision of the movie business and its future was somewhat limited. His main interest was in the technical qualities of his films as opposed to their content. The next wave in film history would be written by

Cecil B. DeMille (left) and D. W. Griffith (right) were film directors in the early 20th century. Their work helped shape today's film industry. Here, the two directors chat on the set of Demille's 1929 movie, *Dynamite*.

the likes of Cecil B. DeMille and D. W. Griffith. These men saw films as a means to tell stories on a grand scale, in a way that had never been done before. One- to two-hour narratives on film are old news to the modern movie-goer, but in the early twentieth century, this type of entertainment was unheard of.

Thomas Edison invented the home projecting kinetoscope, as seen in this photograph, so that schools could show educational films in their classrooms. Unfortunately, Edison was a bit ahead of his time, and the projecting kinetoscope was unsuccessful.

Edwin Porter, who had earlier directed *The Great Train Robbery* for Edison, seemed to know the direction film was headed in, but he left Edison in 1909. After that, the quality of Edison's film suffered, and he couldn't keep up with his competitors.

One idea Edison did pursue was making motion pictures for educational use. In 1910, he began developing the home projecting kinetoscope. The machine hit the market two years later, and Edison worked hard to get his kinetoscopes into schools. Once again, Edison had an early glimpse of the future: he created a small projector that could easily be set up and operated in the home or in the classroom. The idea was more advanced than the technology, though. The talking motion picture hadn't been perfected yet, and this was an obvious problem when it came to making educational films.

Edison had tried to combine sound with moving pictures before. Together with W. L. Dickson he'd developed a device called the "kinetophone" back in 1895. Dickson made a short film of himself playing a violin while two men danced next to him. The film survives to this day and stands as the first motion picture with live sound.

Still, it was a long way from the kinetophone to recording films with images fully synchronized with music and dialogue. Edison put a lot of money and time into this project but he ran into numerous technical problems and, ultimately, failed to generate enough interest among the schools and educators for whom he was creating the system.

A younger Thomas Edison might have seen this project through to the finish, and perhaps the talking motion picture would have joined the already impressive list of his achievements. The aging inventor was able to let go of his film business, though, selling his interests in it in 1918.

## Fighting to the Bitter End

Edison wouldn't let go of the phonograph so easily, though. By the 1920s, Edison's days as a businessman were all but over. His son Charles was taking more of a leadership role in the business and, in 1926, the

In the 1920s, the radio quickly became a popular form of media and sales of radio sets boomed. This 1926 magazine page advertises the Atwater Kent radio.

# The First Radio

Heinrich Hertz first produced and detected radio waves in his laboratory. Italian physicist Guglielmo Marconi began experimenting with these "Hertzian waves" in 1894. Marconi was able to produce and detect the waves over long distances, leading to the development of the radio. After a few successful demonstrations, Marconi obtained a patent, established the wireless telegraph, and opened the world's first radio factory in Chelmsford, England, in 1898.

In this c. 1901 photograph, Marconi is shown with some of the early radio equipment that he developed.

Wizard named Charles the president of Thomas A. Edison, Inc. Throughout this period, he continued fighting hard for his phonograph against its competitors. Ultimately, it was Edison's famous stubbornness and not just his competitive nature that did him in. In 1921, Edison's sales fell off drastically. That year, there were more than 250,000 radio sets in the U.S. By 1922, the number had nearly doubled. The era of the radio was beginning in America. Charles pleaded with his father to get involved. Edison refused, though. He insisted that the sound quality of the radio was inferior and that the radio was just a crazy fad.

*Ultimately, it was Edison's famous stubbornness and not just his competitive nature that did him in.*

The public disagreed. Millions of dollars were spent on the radio, and the new technology soon became a standard household appliance. By the time Edison reconsidered, it was too late. In 1928, the old man finally gave his son permission to shift the company's attention to radio. Just after the great stock market crash of 1929, all production was stopped at the Edison phonograph plant. An important era was coming to an end.

Charles Edison sits by his father during a 1928 radio broadcast.

# CHAPTER 13

# A National Treasure

*I am tired of all the glory. I want to get back to work.*

Even while Edison's businesses slowly declined, the inventor's reputation was greater than ever. Edison stepped away from the lab to enjoy his growing stature as a national treasure. When the prospects of World War I became more certain, Edison was asked to head the Naval Consulting Board, a group designed to investigate new ideas and technologies that could be used in the war. In 1915, he stated that warfare was "more a matter of machines than men." Now Edison had the chance to breathe life into those words, and he threw himself into the work.

The board sorted through numerous ideas offered by both amateur and professional scientists and inventors. Much of the material was far-fetched and impractical, but Edison invested his time in developing a number of different projects involving submarines. The end result of Edison's labors never moved beyond the realm of ideas, but the work stimulated him. What's more, his inclusion in the process showed how highly regarded he was by powerful people in the government.

*What's more, his inclusion in the process showed how highly regarded he was by powerful people in the government.*

# The Next Generation of Innovations

Edison's popularity wasn't limited to the U.S. government. While some of his contemporary scientists may have rejected Edison, a new breed of innovators and entrepreneurs admired him greatly. First and foremost among these was Henry Ford. Ford had worked for the Edison Illuminating Company in Detroit, Michigan, during the 1890s. Edison was his hero, and Ford was delighted when he met the Wizard at an annual company party.

At the time, Ford was working on his first gas-powered engines, and by 1903, he had made enough progress to start the Ford Motor Company. He told Edison about his work, and the great inventor responded enthusiastically. "Young man," Edison

In this c. 1920 photograph, Henry Ford is shown standing in front of his famous Model T car.

# Henry Ford's Model T

Henry Ford was not the first person to work with gas-powered engines, and he wasn't the first to develop a self-propelled gas vehicle, but the introduction of the Model T, in 1908, changed the auto industry drastically and made Ford the most important person working in this field. The Model T had an internal combustion engine and was unlike any car that came before. This car was affordable and easy to operate and maintain. It quickly became a huge success. By 1918, half of all cars in America were Model Ts.

Ford had trouble keeping up with the huge demand for his cars. In response, he pioneered the assembly line, opening up a massive factory in Highland Park, Michigan. Factory workers remained in place, adding one component to each automobile as it moved past them on the assembly line, and the process was carefully timed to keep things moving efficiently. This method of building cars helped Ford sell his Model Ts at an affordable price. As a result, Ford made a huge impact not only on the auto industry but on the whole idea of factory production.

An early assembly line at the Ford factory is shown in this 1913 photograph.

Edison and his friends Harvey Firestone Jr., R.J.H. DeLoach, John Burroughs, Henry Ford, and Harvey Firestone, on a camping trip in Bolar Springs, Virginia, in August 1918.

said, "that's the thing! You have it! Your car is self-contained and carries its own power plant."

With Edison's encouragement, Ford continued to pursue his dream and later introduced the famous Model T, an invention that changed the world every bit as much as Edison's lightbulb had. The two men became great friends. As Edison began spending more time at his home in Fort Myers, Ford visited often, eventually buying the house next door.

Edison developed batteries for the new gas cars and thought of other ways to make a profit in this booming new car industry. At the same time, Ford recruited Edison for a series of all-star camping trips. These trips during the 1920s would also include the tire manufacturer Harvey Firestone, the naturalist Luther Burbank, and, at least once, President Warren G. Harding.

*Ford continued to pursue his dream and later introduced the famous Model T.*

Edison sometimes brought Mina along on these famous expeditions, and he always had great fun, enjoying his role as the group's father figure.

## A Far-Reaching Legacy

Ford also helped ensure that Edison's legacy would endure for ages by setting up an elaborate museum in his hometown of Dearborn, Michigan. Ford's goal was to tell the story of America to everyone. Edison and his legacy played a big part in that story. Ford acquired old tools from Edison's Menlo Park laboratory. He also brought back original pieces of the Menlo Park lab itself and eventually even transported Edison's original Fort Myers workshop, in its entirety, to Dearborn. Ford gathered artifacts from every period of Edison's life. Ford went so far as to ship soil in from the site

Edison's rebuilt lab lives on in the Ford Museum, photographed here in 1929.

of Edison's New Jersey lab. His creation would eventually be named the Edison Institute.

Ford opened the museum in 1929 with a grand tribute to Edison called Light's Golden Jubilee. The jubilee celebrated Edison's invention of the lightbulb and his stature as a great American inventor. The Menlo Park lab was completely reconstructed for the event, which was carried live on the radio. Old assistants, including Francis Jehl, joined Edison in a dramatic re-enactment on the famous night they had first succeeded in lighting one of their bulbs.

The event involved plenty of fanfare. Newly elected President Herbert Hoover was in attendance and comments by physiscist Albert Einstein were piped in by radio. The great inventor's legacy had been secured. Still, Edison himself looked tired. He was coming to the end of a fruitful life, and he'd had enough of the spotlight. "I am tired of all the glory," he said. "I want to get back to work."

## The Final Years

However, most of Edison's work was behind him. In 1921, he had resigned from the Naval Board, frustrated with the lack of progress he had made in advancing his ideas. Edison often clashed with younger scientists who thought his methods were outdated, and he grew tired of the difficulty of getting the government to approve his

Thomas Edison celebrated his eighty-fourth birthday with his wife, Mina, on February 11, 1931—about eight months before his passing.

Even though Edison survived on very little sleep during his most inventive years, he occasionally took a nap in his later years. In this 1921 photo, he is shown resting under a tree during a camping trip with President Harding in the Blue Ridge Mountains.

projects. Charles had essentially been running the company in his father's absence, and continued to do so after Edison's return. The Wizard would never be able to stop working completely, but his most productive days were past.

While Edison had never been the most attentive father, he'd become the patriarch of a great clan. In 1925, his youngest son, Theodore, was the last Edison child to be married. The Wizard saw his first grandchild, born to daughter Madeleine and her husband, John Eyre Sloane, in 1916. By 1931, the Sloanes had provided Edison with three more grandchildren.

In two years, Edison had been honored by two presidents. In 1928 he received an honorary medal from President Coolidge, who called him a "benefactor of mankind." The next year he was praised by President Hoover at Light's Golden Jubilee. Edison was the head of a large family and owned a reputation as one of America's most important men. What more was left for the great inventor to do?

# A Final Pursuit

Unsurprisingly, Thomas Edison spent the last few years of his life chasing one last great invention. The Model T had started an automobile craze in this country, and later across the world. Finding cheap rubber for automobile tires was quite difficult, but Edison, encouraged by Ford and Firestone, was determined to find a way to do it.

Edison did a lot of his rubber research at his Florida home, where he had dedicated several acres to growing plants that might prove a good source of natural rubber. Some rubber was grown in the United States, but most of it was being imported from South America. Edison began serious research in 1927, organizing the Edison Botanic Research Corporation, and a few years later he thought he'd arrived at a solution. He decided that goldenrod was the ideal plant for growing and extracting rubber, and began to think about launching a large-scale **extraction** operation.

Edison thought the goldenrod plant could be used to produce rubber. He displays the giant plant in this c. 1927 photograph.

We don't know how successful Edison's rubber explorations would have been. Goldenrod seemed like a promising natural source for rubber, but synthetic rubber was becoming a factor in the rubber trade, and its importance would increase. At any rate, the great inventor was running out of time. In 1931, Edison filed his 1,093rd U.S. patent. It would be his last.

By September 1931, Edison had become quite ill. He had developed diabetes late in life and was also having serious trouble with his kidneys. Edison continued getting weaker and weaker. Finally, on October 18, the great Thomas Edison died.

The whole world mourned Edison's death. Mina had his casket kept open for two days at Edison's West Orange laboratory, and thousands of people came to pay their respects. On the evening of his funeral, Americans were asked to dim their electric lights for one minute, in tribute to the great inventor who had brought light into the world.

Edison's body lies in state in the library of his home in Glenmont, New Jersey.

# Glossary

**alternating current**—a type of electric current that reverses its direction at regular intervals.

**capitalize**—to get the most value out of a given thing or situation.

**compulsive**—driven by powerful, irresistible urges or motivations.

**conjured**—brought forth through imagination or the appearance of magic.

**corrosion**—process of destruction by chemical action.

**current**—the flow of electrical charge between two points.

**dynamo generator**—a machine that converts energy into the form of electric currents and uses those currents to power lights and lighting systems.

**eclipse**—phenomenon whereby the light of a luminous body, such as the sun or the moon, is obscured by another heavenly body.

**exposition**—a large public display or exhibition.

**extraction**—process of drawing or pulling something out.

**filament**—a tiny threadlike fiber.

**gaslights**—lighting fixtures that produce illumination by the burning of gas.

**incandescent lightbulb**—a glass globe with a white-hot filament inside that gives off light and is typically powered by electricity.

**Industrial Revolution**—a time period during the late eighteenth and early nineteenth centuries when there was a rapid development of machines and power tools.

**patents**—exclusive rights obtained by individuals, or groups of people, to pursue specific processes, inventions, or products.

**projectors**—machines with a light source and an internal system of lenses used to display enlarged images on a screen.

**railroad baron**—one of a small group of wealthy tycoons who financed and controlled the growth of the American railroad during the nineteenth century.

**revolutionized**—changed or made a dramatic difference.

**Stock Exchange**—a marketplace for the buying and selling of stocks or shares of monetary investments.

**technology**—the application of scientific research and innovation in the industrial or mechanical arts.

**ventures**—business opportunities that run the risk of great economic loss or gain.

**visionary**—a person with new ideas and an insight into the future.

**voltage**—the force of electrical current that is measured in volts.

# Bibliography

Baldwin, Neil. *Edison: Inventing the Century*. New York: Hyperion Books, 1995.

Clark, W. Ronald. *Edison: The Man Who Made the Future*. New York: G.P Putnam's Sons, 1977.

Guthridge, Sue. *Thomas A. Edison: Young Inventor*. New York: Aladdin, 1949.

Israel, Paul. *Edison: A Life of Invention*. New York: John Wiley, 1998.

Jehl, Francis. *Menlo Park Reminiscences*. New York: Dover, 1990.

Jonnes, Jill. *Empires of Light: Edison, Tesla, Westinghouse, and the Race to Electrify the World*. New York: Random House, 2003.

King, C. David. *Thomas Alva Edison: The King of Inventors*. Auburndale, Massachusetts: History Compass, 1997.

Moran, Richard. *Executioner's Current: Thomas Edison, George Westinghouse, and the Invention of the Electric Chair*. New York: Knopf, 2002.

Pretzer, William. *Working at Inventing: Thomas A. Edison and the Menlo Park Experience*. Baltimore, Maryland: Hopkins University Press, 2002.

Wachhorst, Wyn. *Thomas Alva Edison: An American Myth*. Cambridge, Massachusetts: The MIT Press, 1983.

# Image Credits

# About the Author

Martin Woodside grew up in Brooklyn, New York. He holds an MA in English from the University of California at Davis and is currently working on an MFA in creative writing at San Diego State University. He's completed three abridgements for Sterling Publishing's Classic Starts series—*Tom Sawyer*, *Gulliver's Travels*, and *The Wind in the Willows*. He is now working on a fourth, *Arabian Nights*.

# Index